R. F. O. Kemp.

HOUSEHOLD
AND
COUNTRY
CRAFTS

HOUSEHOLD
AND
COUNTRY
CRAFTS

ALLAN JOBSON

LONDON **ELEK** NEW YORK

Printed in Great Britain by
Page Bros. (Norwich) Ltd
Norwich

FOREWORD

THIS book is the outcome of a private museum made by the author and his wife, and owes much to other collections both public and private. Especial thanks are due to Mr. and Mrs. Parker of Tickenhill Manor, Bewdley, Worcestershire, and the valuable help gained from their collection. The information has come directly from the various practitioners in their respective arts, who so gladly gave of their lore. Some of the matter has appeared in *Country Life*, and the author's indebtedness for permission to reproduce is gratefully acknowledged.

CONTENTS

ILLUSTRATIONS

*The illustrations are made up of examples of imple-
ments and products of craftsmanship and are listed
here under the chapters to which they refer.*

ONE

THE KITCHEN

*"A good coke is half a physysyon. For the chefe physyche . . .
doth come from the Kytchyn."*

BORDE, 1542.

THE spacious days of the Kitchen have passed, indeed
the kitchen itself is no more, superseded by the
kitchenette, the tin-opener and the ration book. From
time immemorial it flourished, even on into Edwardian
days, and then by wars and lack of domestic help it
passed in the general change of life. Yet in its earlier
history, when wealth was reckoned in possessions and
kind, since there was but little money, it called forth
architectural triumphs such as those seen at Stanton
Harcourt, Oxon, with a domed roof; the Abbot's Kitchen
at Glastonbury, square on plan, with four fireplaces at
the angles, making it an octagon, each capable of roasting
an ox; the Bishop's Palace, Durham; Raby Castle; and
Bamburgh Castle. In each of these examples the kitchen
is a detached building, connected with the main building
by passages, leading to the screen in the Great Hall,
and so designed in all probability to minimise the danger
from fire.

And since these buildings catered for so many, the
enormous number of retainers and the equally surprising
number of visitors (since travelling was so difficult), so
they called forth an immense array of equipment that
varied according to the locality and the methods
employed, based on centuries of tradition. Spits, screens,

jacks; and a table, the top of which would consist of a
solid plank of oak, some great denizen of the forest that
lengthened out its years in the service of many cooks.
Yet with all the plenitude, a fine economy prevailed, not
preached but practised.

The houseproud woman of those years was one
entirely different from that understood by the term today.
She was one who, if not actively engaged in the kitchen
herself, supervised in no uncertain way all that went on
therein. The kitchen was indeed the hub of the house,
and reflected in its labours the temper of the household.
Besides catering for those beneath its own roof, it spoke
of hospitality, a prized and cherished expression of the
art of living.

The economy was truly remarkable, not only providing
for the moment and the next meal, but always with an
eye to tomorrow. The surplus of butter in the summer
was laid down in huge pans for the winter. Eggs were
either pickled or placed in hoops that could be moved
slightly once a week, causing each egg to roll over and so
prevent the yolks from sticking to the shells. Apples
were peeled, cut into rings, and hung on long strings to
dry, while the grapes were dried and made into raisins.
Nuts were put into large earthenware jars, covered over
with leaves and put into the ground, and the various
herbs were dried for seasoning.

Most careful accounts were kept as evidenced by the
Household Book of Dame Alice de Bryene (1412–1413),
which shows the whole management of the household
of a great lady in the time of Agincourt, giving the
number who were fed at her table, and exactly what
they ate down to the last pigeon and herring. For
example an old pipe which had contained wine, was
turned into three keelers (tubs) for the bakehouse. The

sharpening of the kitchen knife is duly recorded, as is the purchase of earthen pans to catch the dripping, a strainer at two-pence, and a pestle at the same price.

That this gear was highly prized is evidenced by old wills, for example in that of Richard Purdy, 1498, which includes: 'ij great bras pottis and i lasser pot, v pewter platers, v pewter dishes, v pewter sawcers w^t myn other trene vessels, ii spetis, an anndern, a gredy (gridiron), ewyer, ij Truets, a spruse hutche, a jointed cofir, a salt tabill iij trestles, iij fourmes, a pile of iron a bason w^t an ewer of laton, a chafyng bason, my best carwdrun, a kitch, a fraune of vi galons, and a maser of silver and gilt the bond. . . .'

Wooden implements loomed large, scoured as clean as drift-wood, supplied by the cooper and the wood-turner or the village carpenter. These included various tubs and vats for salting and storing meat, churns and casks, flour-bins and meal tubs. The turnery included all kinds of interesting and useful articles made chiefly of sycamore as this wood does not affect the colour or taste of food; such as wooden spoons, bowls, egg cups, butter-prints, rolling or paste-pins, and boards, stools and various handles, butter scales. A spoon with a twist in the handle called a Welsh Gamm spoon, is said to have been specially made for a man of that name who had a twisted mouth and is thought to have originated the term 'gammy', now applied to a crooked leg. The turner would also be responsible for the pestle and mortar, cut from the solid, in this case used for pounding meat when making minces and potted meats (*Fig.* 6).

The potter, who presided over the local brick kells, reserved his 'best earth' for those old red earthenware vessels, so beautiful in colour and texture, and so much in demand (*Fig.* 25). They were often of greater moment than the iron or copper pots because in old kitchens a great deal of vinegar was used, either wine vinegar or malt vinegar (formerly known as alegar), and verjuice; strong acids that would have reacted on metal. One wonders if they were in part responsible for the then fatal complaint of gout in the stomach.

There were deep basins for kneading the dough, common to almost all parts, but these pots varied with the locality. There were the Bread Mugs of Cumberland, large, deep jars about twenty-four inches high, fitted with a lid, in which the bread was stored; the huge fireproof basins in which the bread was baked, known as Punks in Durham, Joles in Staffordshire, and Bowles (rhyming with fowls), in Yorkshire; and Buckly-pans used for storing butter in the hill farms of Wales. At Bideford they made Fish-Stains of three sizes—great crocks, buzzards and gallons—in which the pilchards were pickled; and at Barnstaple they produced pitchers named according to size—Long Tom, Ferret Tail, Gully Mouth, Punch Gut, Sixties and Penny Joog; while Dorsetshire provided Pills, in all of which the thrower could express his genius in just that little difference.

Huge iron pots were slung over the fire by means of cranes or hakes (gantry in North Wales), because a good deal of boiling was done, and there was always something simmering in their cavernous depths. When cooking vegetables, the various kinds were put in nets and boiled up together, and no soda was used, as the cooking water was fed to the swill tubs for the pigs. On the other hand, large amounts of food such as for Harvest Suppers and Christmas were boiled in the copper. Saucepans in the early days were merely used as their name implies, for the decoction of sauce. Later there came the lidded-pots as illustrated (*Fig. 5*), which were evidently early examples of pressure cookers. These digestive pots have lids which fasten on by grooves over lugs, and vent holes are provided in the centre of the lid.

Then there was a goodly array of spits, roasters and branders in shining steel, without which no kitchen was complete. These were manipulated sometimes by a smoke-jack driven by a draught made by the fire as it roared up the chimney, but usually by a chain that ran over a pulley wheel to which a weight was attached wound up by a winch. Meat thus cooked rivalled in flavour anything produced by our modern ovens, as the juices were held inside the carcase or joint by reason of a baked skin forming on the outside. Mutton was a delectation when it arrived on the table from such a source. And here in passing is a recipe for Suffolk gravy: 'Baste the meat well with the dripping and about an hour before the meal put $\frac{3}{4}$ cup of boiling water into the latch-pan, dredge in some flour and keep basting every ten minutes. Five minutes before the meal is served add a little more boiling water if required, and set the pan on the top of the stove to simmer, when it will brown and thicken.'

The tin roasting-jack, meat screen, or hastener (surely a happy term for a hungry stomach agitated by the smell), carried on the tradition. The one on the left of Figure 3 has a clockwork cylinder causing the hook to revolve backwards and forwards. They were picturesque if cumbersome appliances of the kitchen now quite obsolete. In cottages, where such an expensive item was not possible, the meat was suspended in front of the fire by string and fastened to a gimlet or a nail driven into the mantel-shelf. The tin-smith-made oven and clockwork spit is light and portable, and must have been an excellent addition to the kitchen equipment. It is complete with latch-pan.

The kitchen was often the most comfortable part of the house; indeed there were often two of them, a back kitchen where the work of preparation was done, and a front where meals were served. Here the men folk came in their boots and found comfort for their feet. It was to such a place that the immortal Pickwickians came when they arrived at Dingley Dell, and Mr. Pickwick's boots were brushed on his feet until his corns were red hot. If the men were field workers, there would be a jar of Neat's-foot oil, supplied by the butcher, to daub over the leather and keep out the wet. If the boots thus treated were held before the fire they gave forth a smell sufficient to disturb the most stubborn nose. Blacking-skins were a messy business, but a patent bracket helped in holding the boot firm at such a height as best suited the cleaner. And when the good man retired for the night, he probably placed his boots carefully near the hearth, heel to toe, to ensure a good night's rest, and as a guard against the cramp.

The kitchen in the Westmorland farms was the principal room in the house, very low pitched, with huge oak beams crossing the ceiling. The floor was covered with large square-shaped thick slate flags, or paved with cobbles from the nearest beck; sometimes it was of beaten earth. The fireplace was funnel-shaped, three or four yards in diameter and occupied a large portion of the room, the hearth being raised a few inches above the floor. A large beam, known as the rannel-balk, crossed the chimney at the upper floor level, and from this the rattan-crook was suspended by a chain. This could be adjusted as required for cooking.

These open chimneys were somewhat murky places, as in wet weather the water trickled down the sides creating a black slime that adhered to everything it came in contact with. It was known as the hallen-drop. The fire was of peat or wood and never allowed to go out because of the great trouble in rekindling it; it was kept alight from generation to generation. In the recesses by the fire were two long settles, and in the long winter evenings the family congregated here, carded wool, span and knitted stockings according to custom. From the rannel-balk, as also at the sides of the chimney, hung the beef, mutton and bacon which had been killed in the fall, about Martinmas, because of the lack of provender; the pigs being killed from Christmas to Candlemas. This dried meat had to serve the household until early summer.

A passage called the hallan separated the kitchen from the bower where the master and mistress slept, and from the mell, or dairy. Behind the kitchen was the down-house, which was a single storied building where the fire-elding was kept, and where the brewing and baking was done.

Pottery both for use and ornament would be found in the kitchen, perchance a puzzle-jug to entrap the stranger into trying his skill at drinking some of the contents without spilling it through the holes in the neck. Actually the liquid is sucked up through the handle and out by one of the spouts in the rim. It takes its place with the fuddle-cups of the period. Then comes a bellarmine, or grey-beard bottle, so named from Cardinal Robert Bellarmine, born in Tuscany in 1542. He was hated by the Protestants of the Low Countries because of his persecution of the reformed religion. These common ale-pots retaliated by caricaturing his appearance:

Thou Thing,
Thy belly looks like to some strutting hill
O'ershadowed with thy rough beard like a wood.

2

Next to this in the illustration (*Fig.* 7), is a Sussex harvest bottle of pleasant shape, which may hail from Cadborough near Rye, Chailey or Burgess Hill. Then follows a cider or beer flagon in the shape of a smiling brewer's drayman's head. He is wearing the traditional maltster's cap, seen fifty years ago not only at the maltings, but also in the London streets, when they replenished the pub cellars. The ringed pottery mugs were common to farmhouse kitchens, as also the Fulham-ware mug in the centre.

And what kitchen mantel-pieces would have been complete without the spice boxes or the spice mills? There is one of these in Figure 4 like the leaning tower of Pisa, which is an interesting example of the wood-turner's art in that all the boxes are separate and screw into one another, and have transfer labels on each. Neither must we omit the hour-glass that found a place in every kitchen. These glasses served, not only to time the cooking, as the one on the left in Figure 8, which marks quarter, half and three-quarter hours, but were veritable time-pieces as well, for the one, centre, takes four hours to run out. And it was by an hour-glass that the labourers timed their meals.

Incidentally, someone writing of farmhouse life in 1865, before living-in was entirely abandoned, remarked that the kitchen would be innocent of tea and sugar except on baking days, though meat was eaten at both breakfast and dinner. Supper was mainly bread and milk eaten with wooden spoons from well scoured wooden platters and it was no unusual thing to rectify the jagged edge of a spoon at table with the clasp-knife.

The fire-crane or hake was familiar to most kitchen hearths, and is a proud product of the blacksmith, (*Fig.* 1). It exhibits the twist beloved by that craftsman, and has three movements. It sways backwards and forwards, the kettle can be raised or lowered by placing the bar under the notches as required, and the hook can be moved along the top rail. With this, left, is a salamander for browning off pastry and cakes by making it red hot and holding it over the crust. It was also used before the blow-lamp by decorators. Boys would hold it over old paint while the workman scraped off the seared skin of paint. Below is a beer muller, which thrust into the embers of the fire took the chill off the beer; it is also known as a dandy in East Anglia and a devil in Hereford.

The rack with rings is a pipe-rack, burner or cleaner. The long clays were placed in this after use, and the whole was put into the fire or stood in the brick oven overnight, and came out as good as new in the morning. It reminds us that many old houses possessed special pipe-cupboards in which to store the pipes, which were bought in quantities, such as a gross, or in barrels. Hawkers, who had special 'pipe-walks', were the sellers.

Sugar was then supplied in loaf or cone form that looked much like a dunce's cap. These weighed 14 pounds, stood 30 inches high, and were 7 inches at the base. Containers are preserved in Lavenham Church, Suffolk, where sugar was first made from beet in 1868. They were in use until 1874. This loaf sugar called forth a large array of nippers to deal with it. First the cone was broken up by the chopper, and then various nippers, with or without stands, broke it up still further for use at table (*Fig.* 4).

Old farmhouses often had a grape-vine on the west or south side walls, which generally succeeded in ripening in the gay old summers, producing a small sweet grape. They have curiously disappeared in these modern times. Grape wine figured large amongst the various distillations

that took place in the kitchen, and was greatly esteemed.
Here then is a recipe which comes from Suffolk: 'To
28 lbs of bruised grapes add 3 gallons of cold water,
let it stand three or four days, stirring occasionally.
Strain it, add 18 lbs of preserving sugar, strain it through
a piece of muslin, put it into bottles or barrel, when
finished working add ½ oz isinglass, let it stand till March,
then bottle, taking care to secure the corks with string
or wire.'

The copper, indeed there might be more than one,
was of that metal and not zinc as in these later days. It
was scoured clean and shone, a proud possession since
it served for brewing, cooking, wine making, and not
merely for washing. The brick or stone floor of the
kitchen was washed once a week, and rubbed over with
another brick to act as a scourer, and then sanded. This
sand was often peddled at the door by some poor old
dame, in a wooden hod like that used by the stone
pickers, at a half-penny a hod. Then as a final flourish,
the broom was drawn over the floor in sweeps, making a
pattern of semi-circles in the loose sand, and there might
be a bundle of wheat-straw at the door for the men folk
to wipe their feet on coming in from the muddy yard.

In striking contrast to the vast array as detailed above
in kitchen equipment, came the simple requirement of the
old-fashioned Scottish hind, which was limited to three
things, all or any of which could be hung over the
'swey'. This was a long chain dangling over the peat
fire with a hook on the end. First, the tea-kettle, then the
'yetlin' or porridge pot, with third, the girdle. On the
latter they made oatcakes, and barley bannocks, which
were made from peas and barley; also girdle scones of
flour and milk. With the kettle they made brose, by
pouring hot water into a basin of oatmeal, stirring the

while, and adding a pat of butter. Bread was made by covering the loaves with clay, and thrusting them into the fire.

This kind of simple diet persisted in the North of England, where the women field workers maintained a hard and strenuous life on the wholesome diet of oatmeal porridge and milk. They were noted for their lovely complexions, with clear eyes, good skins, and a healthy open-air colour derived from exposure to wind and sun. But when they abandoned their traditional diet for tea and white bread, their physique and appearance deteriorated.

Adjacent to the kitchen would be the Still-Room or Still-House, in which the ladies would busy themselves making all kinds of waters, cordials, medicines and juleps for household and village use in illnesses. The equipment for this apartment is well shown in the Inventory of Hengrave Hall, Suffolk, dated 1603.

Itm. one great brasse pot to still with.
Itm. V Skellets of brasse.
Itm. one lymbick of tinne.
Itm. two great mortars, with pestalls to them.
Itm. one greate panne of latten with a furnace of iron to hould fier in.
Im. iiij moulds of tinne to make bisket cakes.
Itm. vj white earth pannes to preserve in.
Itm. one basket to keep march panes in.
Itm. one cradell of iron to roast appells on.
Itm. one little rounde deep maunde for herbs. (maunde = hand basket).
Itm. three pair of wafer irons.
Itm. ij mustard mills.
Itm. one sheet to keep roses in.

Itm. one little coffer with lock and keye for spice bread.

Itm. one borded chest to keep fruit in.

Itm. Gallypots and other pots for conserves.

Itm. Six Venice banquetting dishes.

Figure 2 shows one of these appliances, which is probably part of an apparatus for distilling aromatic waters. 'In the kitchen one pewter still, in the room next the parlour, one pewter limbeck', which latter is an obsolete West-Country word for vessels for distilling liquors, and is a contraction of alembic.

Here too, might be found the gingerbread moulds (*Fig.* 9), which were also used for pastry and marzipan, as also presumably marchpanes. They are cut intaglio out of the solid, some being double-sided, and are beautifully executed. Apart from their use in the kitchen, gingerbreads were, of course, distinguishing features at country fairs, existing from quite early days, for they were common in the reign of Henry IV. At first, ginger-bread was made with honey and gilded with gold leaf. Later Dutch leaf replaced English and was wont to tarnish, hence the expression—'taking the gilt off the gingerbread'. It is curious to note how these old customs died, for at Horsham, Sussex, a noted gingerbread was produced that was in great favour in 1866 but by 1890 it had completely died out.

With these too, would go the pastry jigs and cutters for marking designs on the pastry, and pressing down the edge on to the dish giving it a frilly appearance (*Fig.* 4).

Old Inventories and Household Books are fruitful sources for information respecting obsolete terms and items of interest. This from a Mrs. Pearle's *Account Book and Diary*, 1701, records a now long-since departed object of the kitchen: 'Oct. 1705. Mending ye striking bord, 8d.'

It appears this was a large board some six feet long, by three feet wide, which was laid over a table, usually smaller than that, upon which a batch of bread was kneaded or worked up into loaves. When not in use for that purpose it could be used as an ironing board.

TWO

BAKING IN THE OLD
BRICK-OVENS

OLD brick-ovens, sometimes called stick-ovens, and as far as I can gather, also known as kilns in East Anglia, were responsible for centuries of excellent and prolific bakings carried out once a week, or sometimes fortnightly. As with all these domestic happenings, it was a happy and almost sociable business, performed not as a drudgery but as a pleasant and necessary routine; one with the churning, brewing and washing that made up the tale of the year. Great art, and a great knowledge based on long traditions, went into its practise. All those who recall the products of these ovens are unanimous in their verdict that nothing tasted sweeter than the things baked in this manner (*Fig.* 10).

The implements used were a two-tined fork made of wrought-iron, not steel as for field work, to handle the faggots; and a peel which served to place the articles in position and also to remove the ashes or shovel them to one side (*Fig.* 11). Sometimes a hoe came in handy for withdrawing the ashes, or a raffling-pole of sere wood. The wing of a bird was used to sweep the ashes from the oven's mouth.

First the faggots, known also as kilnware, had to be got ready to serve as kindling for the oven, more often than not cut from furze bushes. At Southwold in Suffolk, these were cut from the Common and tied up in small bundles, for which the cutter got a half-penny, the Corporation of Southwold a farthing, and the carter a farthing, making a penny in all. And, most important of all, the oven had to be of the right heat to produce successful results. How, then, was this gauged, since these faggots might be wet or dry according to the weather and the season? If they were wet, firing would take longer to heat, and the oven might be hot at one end yet cool near the entrance. It was almost a case of instinct, for there was no question of thermometers.

It should be realised that the oven bricks were clean and light in colour as left from the previous baking, and one old lady who had followed the practice for years explained the secret. If soot could be seen on the bricks it was a sure sign that the heat was not enough, but so soon as this was burnt off and a general glow appeared on the red bricks, then was the time to 'slop the thing in', as she termed it—'slop' possibly being a corruption of slip. Sometimes a little flour was thrown in; if it turned brown the oven was ready.

The dough was set some hours beforehand, sometimes the previous evening. A great earthenware pan was used, into which a stone or more of flour was emptied with a little salt added. Then a hole was made in the centre of the flour, and a tablespoonful of yeast, mixed with a little luke-warm milk, was dropped into the opening. The flour was then gradually mixed until the yeast was covered. Now some warm skim-milk or water was added and the whole worked or kneaded by hand until the right consistency was gained. The dough was then covered with a warm cloth and left to rise. This was known as 'laying the sponge'. In the case of poorer households, mashed potatoes were used as an ingredient. Care had to be taken all through the process to see that the dough was kept warm, for which purpose it was usually placed on the right-hand side of the hearth, or on the copper if that was in use. It was often sealed with the sign of the Cross. Yeast was saved from the brewing for this purpose, preserved in large stone jars with a little clean water run in on top.

Next the dough was placed on the pastry-board, cut up in suitable portions, put in baking tins, and transferred to a moderate oven to bake for an hour, the precaution having been taken to slash the loaves across their tops with a knife. This marking was more or less individual, and must not be changed, or else bad luck would come. Cottage-loaves were placed directly on the hot floor of the oven, without tins, the wood-ash having been dusted away, and they were considered the sweetest bread of all. In some cases before the bread had finished baking it was taken out and a mixture of egg and milk was quickly brushed over its top crust to give it a glaze. Needless to say, some skill was required in landing the bread, balanced on the end of the peel, and disengaging the peel without disturbance of balance. This must have been especially difficult with rice-puddings and fluid dishes. The bread was usually baked in one operation, and by itself, as the opening and closing of the oven door was apt to send it heavy or *sad*; in no case must the oven door be slammed. It was unlucky to bake an odd number of loaves and short-cakes, or to make an uneven number of pricks in a biscuit.

The order of procedure was as follows: First, short-cakes, tarts, buns, rusks and all small articles. Then, sausage-rolls, meat-pies, fruit-tarts, milk-puddings, potato-puddings (made of potatoes, slices of fat pork, onions, with or without a pastry crust, very delicious for tea on baking day, usually a Friday), beef-puddings baked in batter, and apples done likewise; and last of all the bread.

As the bread was made from stone-ground flour from the local mill it was darker than our roller-ground variety, and as it was leavened with yeast instead of baking-powder, it would keep moist for a week or more. And it is interesting to recall that it was with the advent of the roller-ground flour that people's teeth became affected, proof of which is to be found in old skulls dug up with wonderful sets of teeth. To eat new bread was considered an extravagance, and one old lady of my acquaintance who died a centenarian was wont to bake 26 loaves a week, but always kept back six from the previous bake. Should the yeast happen to be sour—and it was easily affected by thundery weather—then it was most unfortunate for the household, as, since the economy of those days forbade waste, they were doomed to eat sour or *mothery* bread for a week. Evidently this was in the mind of Wycliffe when he translated: 'Beware of the sour dough of the Pharisees,' using that word instead of leaven. It also passed into a Suffolk proverb, and 'Come to bad bread', is given by Edward FitzGerald in his *Sea Words and Phrases* as typifying 'to come worse off, whether by word or other usage'. This, happily, was the exception, and the batch of bread as it was withdrawn from the oven gave off a delicious smell that lingers as a happy memory with some elderly people. It might be mentioned that *ocketts of bread* were the first and last crusts, and the *kissing* crusts were those between two loaves, a delicacy much sought after by the younger members of the family.

An essential article of kitchen furniture in those times was the hutch for storing the flour; a large coffer-like piece with shelving sides, set on legs, often of oak or elm, now sought after as an antique. These are sometimes mentioned in old wills as a 'mynging-trough', from 'ming or myng- to mix as in the case of dough'. One or two sayings grew up about this, to 'mung the miller's eye out', was to overdo the mixture with too much fluid when making the dough.

One or two tasty viands were derived from the weekly bake, and were said to be 'off the dough', or 'off the bread'. The chief was rusks. For these a lump of dough was put in a basin. To 2 pounds was added 2 ounces lard, 2 ounces butter and 2 eggs. These ingredients were all worked well by the hands and moistened with milk if necessary, then sprinkled with flour and left for a time. The mixture was then broken down again, or stiffened up, rolled out flat on the pastry-board to an inch thick, cut out to biscuit shape and baked in the oven on a flat tin for thirty minutes. They were then taken out, split open and returned to the oven to dry off. These rusks were most acceptable for soaking in tea by old people and invalids, as they were more soluble than rusks made with baking-powder. One old custom was to sprinkle sugar over the rusk when it rose to the surface in the tea. Rusks, of course, are still a country delicacy, made as the fat ration will allow.

Another speciality, made only at the season indicated, was the harvest-cake or biscuit, also known as a bever cake. For this a portion of dough was taken off the bread and put in a basin, with lard, two eggs, sugar, raisins, candied peel and nutmeg. These were all thoroughly mixed by hand and left for a time, then baked in a tin, either in biscuit form or as a slab. In some cases egg was brushed over the surface and sprinkled with sugar, then the cake was returned to the oven to be browned off. This was a most welcome addition to the 'fourses' provided by the farmer's wife for the harvest field.

Dumplings were also made of the dough (in fact, flour was known colloquially in Norfolk as *Dumpling Dust*); pieces about the size of a woman's fist were broken off and boiled for twenty-five minutes in salted boiling water. They were excellent with rich gravy from the joint. Then there were swimmers or floaters, made from a portion of dough rolled flat and cut in pieces about the size of a tea saucer, and the thickness of a crumpet. They were slid into the boiling water, and served to take the edge off an appetite, as they were eaten before the meat with treacle or sugar.

Fatty-cake was another form, made from a lump of dough rolled out flat, then spread with lard, sprinkled over with sugar, and doubled over. This rolling out, larding, sugaring, and doubling over, was repeated several times before shaping the dough into a cake for the oven. Dough was also shortened down with lard to make crusts for chicken or meat pies.

One or two customs survived in baking. Good Friday Bread was a small loaf of wheaten-flour, marked with a cross and baked on the morning of Good Friday. It had to be well baked, then kept until the following year, and it was reputed never to go mouldy. It was not intended to be eaten but was administered as a medicine.

In Suffolk it was for long considered lucky to keep Fairy Loaves (fossils of the sea-urchin), on the hob, as these ensured that the house so equipped would never lack bread. I know a cottage where this custom prevails, and they are black-leaded with the rest of the fireplace.

And here is a recipe for making wig or wiggs, which Mr. Pepys refers to—'April 8, 1664, Home to the only Lenten supper I have had of wiggs and ale.' This was a bun or cake made very spongy and light.

'To make very good Wigs: Take a quarter of a peck

of the finest flour; rub into it three-quarters of a pound of fresh butter, till it is like grated bread, something more than half a pound of sugar, half a nutmeg, and half a race of ginger grated; three eggs, yolks and whites beaten very well, and put to them half a pint of thick ale-yeast, and three or four spoonfuls of sack; make a hole in your flour, and pour in your yeast and eggs, and as much milk, just warm, as will make it into a light paste; let it stand before the fire to rise half an hour, then make it into a dozen and a half of wigs; wash them over with eggs just as they go into the oven; a quick oven and half an hour will bake them.'

Suffolk had a word which was in common use fifty years ago, viz. 'dannick'. This may have been a corruption of bannock. It was a name given to a small portion of dough taken from the bread, kneaded with sugar, currants and butter; it was then rolled to the same size as the oven peel on which it was laid, and placed in front of the brick oven to toast. The result was a delicious cake, and one often given to children as the result of a promise of a 'dannick for tea', on baking day.

When February was the last month of the year, it was dedicated to Spring Cleaning, with lustrations or purgings from evil influences, that took the form of a procession (hence Procession Way in old estate maps), the aim and object being to banish any hindrances to fertility. On Feb. 17th, was held the Feast of Fornaculia (from *fornax*, an oven), when the oven, the centre of domestic bliss or its curse, was lustrated, followed by the interior of the house. The procession then moved to the site of future crops that would supply the oven, and the boundaries of those crops. From this in widening degree came the 'Beating' of the Bounds.

Times change and customs stale, therefore the attached

bill of a grocer: 'A Syer, near the old Rose and Crown, Sudbury, Suffolk', dated December 5th, 1831, is of considerable interest. It was for the supply of goods to a parson's household—many of the terms being now obsolete.

Raisins 14 lbs at 7d. 8/2; curts 14 lbs at 11d. 12/10; Sugar 2 st. at 6d. 14/-; do. 1 st. at 7d. 8/2; do. 1 st. at 8d. 9/4; 2 loaves do. at 11d. 11/11; a lf sug 10/11½ £1/2/10½; 1 do. at 9d. 7/10½; Yellow soap two sts 18/- £1/5/10½; Mottld soap 1 st. 10/-; Candyd peel 1 lb. at 1/6. 11/6; London dips 3½ doz at 7/6. £1/6/3; do. mlds ½ doz 4/6; C(arolina) rice 14 lbs 7/-. 11/6; ground rice ½ st. 4/1; B. Lead 6 lbs 6/-. 11/1; Rotten stone 4 lbs 2/8; 6 hearthstones 1/6. 10/1; Whiting 1 st. 6d.; 6 B. Bricks 3/-. 3/6; Blacking 6 bott 9/-; F. Salt 2 st. 1/8, 10/8; 1 basket Salt 1/-, Nutmegs ½ 2/8, 3/8; Mace 1/4, cinnamon 1/4, 2/8; cloves 2 ozs 1/4, allspice 2 ozs 4d., 1/8; whole pepper 2 lbs 5/4, Mustd 1 lb 1/8, 7/0; 1 paper starch 4½ lbs 4/6; 1 fine Stilton cheese 12½ at 16d, 16/8, Congou tea 4 lbs at 6/-, £1/4/0; Gunpowder tea 2 lbs at 10/-, £1; Total £12/19/1.

THREE

THE DOMESTIC BREW

Round about, round about,
Maggoty Pie.
My father loves good ale,
And so do I.

THE 'domestic brew' was a half-yearly affair carried out in March and October; it might almost have been described as a festival. In common with baking, washing and churning it was considered as much a pleasure as a task and it called forth willing helpers. Indeed, the brew presaged eventful times ahead, for it was accomplished in March for consumption at haysel and harvest, and in October for Christmas. One or two minor brews might take place between whiles, but these were merely stop-gaps to repair the ravages of thirst.

Before the brewing commenced the vessels had to be thoroughly scalded and cleansed. The casks were first soaked in cold water, then emptied and boiling water substituted, with usually a length of iron chain dropped in, and some walnut leaves. They were then bunged, and trundled about the yard, the chain rolling about inside acting as an abrasive and the leaves as a sweetener. This done and the water drained off, the casks were filled afresh with boiling water and set aside for a time, and when emptied left for 'the wind to get in'. This work was done by the 'backus-boy', who more often than not was a grown man, one past his prime for other and heavier work.

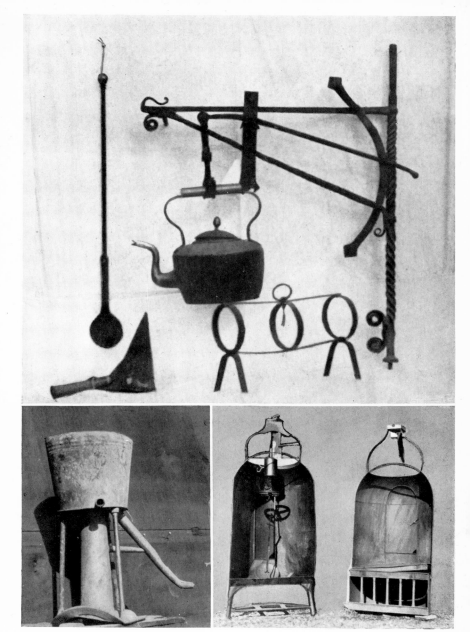

1. Salamander; chimney crane, hake or gantry; beer muller ('devil' in Hereford); pipe burner or cleaner. 2. Pewter still, probably part of an apparatus for the distillation of aromatic waters. 3. Roasting jacks or hasteners (one on left has a clockwork attachment).

THE KITCHEN

4. Bellows, sugar nippers (also at right), turned wood nest of spice boxes, coffee or spice mill, pastry jigs.   5. Stewing pots of metal, probably forerunners of pressure cookers. 6. Wooden pestle and mortar, cut from the solid.   7. Cider flagon of Nottinghamshire ware (Drayman's head), Sussex harvest bottle, puzzle jug, Bellarmine, old wine or beer flagon.   8. Hour-glasses. The centre one may have been used on board ship as it records four hours, or a watch. One on left dates from the seventeenth century.

9. Ginger-bread moulds. 10. Kitchen range in a farmhouse kitchen: brick oven on left, copper, open fire and Dutch oven on right. 11. Oven peel and fork, Salamander.

12. Beer casks on beer stool, mallet and ratchet or tilter. Mash stick above.   **13.** Beer taps, two wicker wilches alias theads or feads, hand cup, bungs and tap for use in wilches, funnel (tunnel in E. Anglia).

THE DOMESTIC BREW

14. Washing Dolly, also known as Dolly pins, Peggy sticks, Poss sticks. **15.** Washing Dollies (the one on left works by suction; it has holes underneath and water is discharged through openings on top), two tubs with lugs. **16.** *above:* flat, or sad irons, goffering iron and goffering machine. *below:* charcoal iron with bag of coal, box iron.

YESTERDAY'S WASH

17. Labour-saving washing machine on rocker base as shown in the 1862 exhibition.
18. Mangling boards. 19. Washing tray and copper stick, one-piece pegs.

20. Cheese vats with (above left and right) milk strainers. **21.** *above:* Cream pans (tins on left, earthenware on right), cream pot with stirrers on top and skimmer or fleeter above, butter prints, milking stool. *below:* Box churn with half-pint butter measure above, skimmers, butter scales, butter beaters, Scotch hands, milk kettle and measures.

THE DAIRY

22. Cheese press. **23.** Pig-killer's outfit: knife in sheath, flail basket of plaited straw, three buckers or gambrels, two scrapers or scuds, pig's nail extractor, hog-stool with lead plate. **24.** Lard press or sausage-stuffer, meat-chopper, sausage funnels. **25.** Pork pot, ham pan, hog pot.

Brewing utensils, especially casks, were valued possessions and part of the gear of every household. Age helped to mellow them and reacted in turn on the beer, so that second-hand ones were often appreciated. A new couple had of necessity to furnish themselves with new equipment, and in such case paid a visit to the cooper, who was known by that prefix, just as the medical practitioner was 'doctor' or the solicitor 'lawyer' Smith or Brown. It might be Cooper Kent of X, or Cooper Baldry of Y, who would seek to know their requirements and have the greatest satisfaction in supplying them, taking a pride in his workmanship and the goods that bore his name. Down the years it would be, 'Cooper Kent made me that cask', and his name would stick to it until the staves fell apart.

On the other hand they might like him to make them a wooden washing-up bowl, which would be so much more kindly than earthenware for the washing of glass or silver. The cooper was also a drier of hams, smoked by the oak saw-dust and chips derived from the labours of his workshop.

Brewing was usually begun at four p.m. when the malt was emptied into a vessel known as a mash-tub. Mashing, also called 'mishing', was most important, and was done by hand. The greatest care was taken to damp every grain of malt, leaving no surplus moisture in the tub. Two people worked opposite one another, each using his hands with a fan motion, drawing the grains towards him, and then working in reverse. The wet malt was left for twelve hours.

A fresh start was made at four the next morning, when the copper was lit and the water brought to the boil. The grains were well stirred with a wooden implement known as a mash-stick (*Fig.* 12), and were then emptied

into a flattish round tub known as a keeler, which was
set on a stool of sufficient height to provide an upper
and lower deck. The boiling water was then hand-
cupped (*Fig.* 13) out of the copper on to the grains. This
was left for another four hours.

The liquid was then drawn off the keeler, care having
been taken to fix a wicker bottle-like object, known as a
wilch or thead, on the inside of the outlet hole by means
of a looped string passing through the opening, often
wedged tight by means of a piece of cloth (*Fig.* 13).
This prevented the grains from coming out with the
liquid. The beer at this stage was known as sweet wort,
and often given to children as a treat.

Next, the liquid was poured back into the copper, and
a pound of hops, loose, was added for every bushel of
malt, and boiled for an hour. Great care had to be
exercised to prevent the mixture from boiling over, and
the hand-cup was in constant use stirring the hops from
the side of the copper. Sometimes the problem was
solved by putting an earthenware plate into the copper,
or a piece of wood.

The liquid was again returned to the keeler, this time
through a hair sieve which was placed on a rack, also
known as tongs, which spanned the tub. More often
than not this rack was formed from a natural forked
branch of a tree out of the hedgerow, as used by the
thatcher for carrying his yokes of straw or reed. A special
brown sugar was sometimes strewn on the bottom of the
tub, the effect of which was to darken the beer and assist
fermentation. Again the liquid was left to cool, this time
to blood heat. The woman who presided over the brew
would be asked to judge when this temperature was
reached. She would sweep her hand through the beer,
consider in her wise old country way, and say 'yes' or

'no' as the case might be. If 'yes', a pint of yeast (also called burgad in Suffolk), was added, and a little flour sprinkled over the surface and then left for the night. On the other hand she might say 'No, that's too hot, partner; the beer'll bloom if we do that yet!'

During the working, the keeler was covered with mats, but should a young and curious person wish to see, they would be rewarded with the sight of masses of brownish mountain peaks rising into frothy heights.

Next day the yeast was skimmed off the beer by means of skimmers or fleeters as used in the dairy to take off the cream from the milk, and put into stone jars. This yeast came in for the weekly bake, and as the grains were fed to the cows with a view to an increased milk supply, or to the pigs, little or nothing in brewing was wasted. The beer could then be put in the casks, care being taken to see they were not over-filled.

The casks were left a few days for any final working to take place, and the yeast removed as it came out through the bung-hole. When the cask was finally bunged, brown-paper was pasted over the bung-hole and the wind-peg or spigot loosened, otherwise there would be an explosion. After some weeks a little of this beer might be drawn off and placed in bottles for festal occasions.

The above is a description of brewing 'best' (sometimes called 'key') beer, and the process was repeated to obtain the mild, or second beer for every-day consumption. The two brewings followed one another and were accomplished from the same ingredients. Naturally enough, attempts were made to get more than two brewings from the same malt, which received various opprobrious terms, such as: 'Rat-tat, Worse-than-That, Rot-gut, and Pim.' Or, 'Red-hood, Not-quite-so-Good, Teter-cum-tauter

(See-Saw), and Nine-times-worse-than-Water.' These terms seemed to fall into rhyme, as:

> First ale and second ale,
> Second Ale and thin;
> Pip and pap, and worse than that,
> And poor old Pim.

Seven varieties have been known to emerge: Ale, Very Good, Small Beer, Mild, Swick-Swack, Worse-than-That, and Pim. East Anglia had a good description for these brews; they were either 'Arms and Legs', that is with no body, or 'Tangle-leg. Thet git intew yare legs, an' make yare legs fly about afore it git intew yare head'. And Tap-Lap was ordinary beer or the droppings of the tap.

The brewing utensils, other than the casks already mentioned, are of great interest. They were all of wood, except the wicker wilch (also called a thead or fead). The hand-cup and the funnel (also picturesquely known as a tunnel), were cut from a solid piece of wood, the handle of the cup and the spout of the funnel included, presumably turned on the pole-lathe. They are usually black with age and many brewings. The spigots and fawcits are beautifully fashioned, as smooth and finished as a pattern for casting. Then there was the beer, or ale-stool, on which rested the casks, and wedges, or stoppers to keep the casks from rolling, the spile for the vent hole, and tilters to tip the cask as it emptied.

Rainwater was highly esteemed for brewing because of its softness. Malt-Wine was an offshoot of the old brew, consisting of sweet-wort to which stone, also known as barley-sugar, was added. This old form of sugar, which resembled rock-crystals strung together by a string, seems to have entirely disappeared. It could be bought at a very low price and was often given to children as a substitute for sweets.

And here is a recipe for Cock-Ale: 'Boyle a cock when he is dressed in some wort, and if you will a neat's tongue too, and when they are boyled all to bittes, then streine them into the rest of the wort having been three hours well boyled also and well wrought. You must also boil spices, and some raisins also with the meat; then put it in the vessels, and let it stand about 3 weeks after it have done working: then bottle it up and within a week or ten days after it is fitt to drink. Flesh do much quicken and make brisk the ale.' William III is said to have 'preferred cock-ale to any sort of wine'.

And this, to be taken just before bed-time to ensure a good night's rest: 'Heat two pints of ale in the muller (devil in Hereford), with two table-spoonfuls of soft sugar and a few cloves. Pour into a hot jug, add some grated nutmeg, some squares of toast, and a wine-glass of rum.' And it might be mentioned that a jug of beer in East Anglia was divided into three draughts: 'Neckum, Sinkum and Swankum.'

Most of the old country inns brewed their own beer, being provided with ample coppers in the scullery for the purpose. A set of brewing-tackle would go with the house, which would include a beer cooler, which was a wooden trough like a shallow box or tray, five-feet long with sides eight to ten inches high.

At Crondall, Hampshire, in Victorian times stood an old and ancient thatched malt house, with a circular house adjoining in which a horse walked round and round, turning an appliance for grinding the malt. This animal was also used, fitted with a pack-saddle, for taking the malt to outlying houses when the roads were bad.

Until 1914 a cottage of under £12 annual rent required

no licence for brewing, but about that time one costing
9s was imposed, which grew in amount later. This,
coupled with the difficulty of obtaining malt brought
the age-old custom to an end. However, in conclusion,
we might recall the words of Trevisa in 1398: 'Hony
cometh of flowers, sidere of frute and ale of corne.'

FOUR

YESTERDAY'S WASH

Monday fetch water, Tuesday run lye,
Wednesday wash, Thursday dry,
Friday iron, Saturday clean,
Sunday cook dinner for old Joe Green.

IT can be asserted definitely that our ancestors were a dirty lot. In Tudor times apparel that needed washing was of small quantity. Underclothes as we understand them were hardly worn at all although a chemise did figure in the list at this time. The wealthy classes wore velvets, taffetas and rich silks, while the poorer sorts wore coarse woollens, and in both classes next the skin. Nightdresses, if worn, were often of thick coloured fabrics as in the case of that worn by Queen Elizabeth, which was of black velvet, while Anne Boleyn's was of black satin. A linen shirt was quite a distinction and exceedingly rare. It has been suggested that the dyer was more in evidence than the laundress.

Yet there were laundresses, who maybe, worked not often, though when they did labour their task must have been strenuous, and the resultant stench considerable. It is not without significance that a clothes-basket was called a *voider*, as instanced in the L'Estrange Household Accounts: 'Itm pd for a payer of voyder yt my Mr gaffe ye said Sir John. Xd.' These, rammed with 'foul stockings and greasy napkins' must have been well named. In the Household Book of Dame Alice de Bryene (1412–13), where most careful accounts are recorded, an old pipe which had contained wine was turned into a tub for the laundress, while another made two washtubs.

Special liquid to act as a bleacher was prepared, known as buck, a word often used by Shakespeare in this sense, and this came to include the clothes so washed. And the buck-basket was that which held the linen about to be washed. The inventory of the Countess of Bath's effects at Chevington Hall (1562), includes 'in the seller, a bucking tub'.

Washing in those far off days appears to have been done in the streams, or even in the common wells, that provided the drinking water. Usually the clothes were placed in a tub, the washerwoman tucked up her skirts and danced on the buck to loosen the dirt. Otherwise the clothes were beaten on boards or stones. The latter method must have been common to Europe, for some Washing Bats of Russian origin are to be seen in Haslemere Museum. And when the washing was accomplished, the laundress sought the aid of 'sweet powder, sweet herbs', which may have included woodruff, for the 'sweet keeping' of the linen.

Coming to more recent times, to those of our grandmothers, Washing Day was something to be reckoned with. It had not the same pleasant aura about it, as say, brewing, baking and churning. Tempers were apt to be affected by the steamy atmosphere and the suds, and the children kept out of the way or remained in bed as long as possible.

In old farm-houses—those self-contained citadels of wonderful economy—two old women who specialised in this kind of labour, would arrive in the chilly hours, sometimes four o'clock, certainly not later than six, and take charge of the stone-flagged kitchen. Wearing their cap with a valance that draped over the neck, often lavender coloured, and on their feet a pair of pattens (clogs or overshoes of wood, raised from the ground by an iron ring). These kept their feet out of the wet, and clipped musically on the flags. They were a voluble race, and clacked away as they worked, fortified with much tea laced with gin.

As in earlier times, Washing Day had to be prepared for, its pathway made straight. In place of buck, a quantity of lye was made in readiness from the wood-ash that came from the copper, brick-oven, or open fires. A large tub, or keeler, was used for this, across the top of which a forked stick of hazel or maple was placed, such as used by thatchers to carry the yelms. On this rested a wooden receptacle with shelving sides, the bottom pierced with small holes to act as a strainer. This was known as a Leech or Letch. The wood-ash, the whiter the better, was placed within and water poured over it. This, percolating, washed out the alkaline salts, being stirred up to promote the process. The resultant lye was then emptied out of the keeler and again passed through the letch bucket, this time passing through muslin to remove any stray particles of ash. This fluid was used for flannels, childrens' garments, whites, and especially prized pieces of napery.

Very often the linen was bleached prior to the wash. It was soaked, and then spread out wet on the bleaching lawns. This served to remove stains and made the washing easier, but was a laborious task not much favoured by the female staff. Saffron was also used for bleaching, as well as cooking.

Instead of beaters, dollies were used, known also as dolly-pins, peggy-sticks, and in the North, poss-sticks, where they are still in use (*Fig.* 14), while the wooden tubs that were used with them took on those prefixes.

Washing-tubs had wooden hoops, as iron hoops would stain the clothes. Washing-trays were also common (*Fig.* 14). These were about 3 feet 6 inches long, with shelving sides, and a little shelf or pocket in one corner to hold the soap, of which primrose was the favourite. No scrubbing was allowed, but the washing was done on rubbing-boards that were ribbed. Then, separating the articles from the sudges or suds, they were transferred to the copper.

Very little soda, if any, was used, instead all the odd pieces of soap were put into the copper and boiled up with the clothes. These were then rinsed in three waters, the last containing blue, and wrung out. It should be recalled this last process was done by hand as no machines were available, and a good deal of artistry and knack went into it. The clothes were not just wisped up, but pleated into convenient handfuls, and then wrung. To dry, they were laid out on the grass or a convenient hedge, which tended to give them a better colour. But if they were hung out, then it was on stout lines and held with pegs cut from the solid, either of ash or hickory, supplied by the cooper. These, now in their survival, appear as perfect little works of art and craftsmanship, characteristic of the countryside.

Then came laundering, a clean and wholesome process, with nothing of the steam and soap-suds of the wash. And just as the old households made their own washing-lye so they made their own starch. For this old potatoes not fit for human consumption were used, and were grated under water with a coarse grater. The resultant mash was left for 24 hours, then the dirty water strained off, and the deposit set on a tray and dried, producing a very useful and strong starch.

Starching as an art reached England about the middle

of the sixteenth century, brought here by the wife of the Queen's coachman—one Gwyllam Boenen, a Dutchman. Later, a Madame Dingham Van der Plasses set up as a clear starcher in London, and is mentioned by Stowe: 'The most curious wives now made themselves ruffs of cambric and sent them to her to be starched, who charged high prices. Madame also took pupils at £5 each, to teach them the art of starching with setting sticks, struts, and poking sticks made of wood or bone. Another £1 was charged for teaching the making of starch.'

Box-mangles were used, either of the London or Yorkshire pattern, filled with stones and worked by a cranked handle. The clothes were wound round the loose wooden rollers, and over these the loaded box ran backwards and forwards. A cumbersome but effective business that caused the operator to sweat. Large articles such as sheets and blankets needed no further attention, but the hems and frills of clothing required to be finished off with the irons.

A whole armoury of irons was called into use. Goffering and Italian or Tally Irons for the frills and the flounces. And for the smoothing, Flat or Sad Irons, box-irons with heaters inside, and charcoal-burning irons (*Fig.* 16).

Of the heaters it is interesting to note that these have given their name to fields and pieces of land in East Anglia that resemble them in shape. The *heater-piece* or the *heater field* for a triangular portion of land is still a common expression. The charcoal irons are still in use in the remote parts of Cumberland, where bags of fuel for domestic use can still be purchased. A little of the coal was placed on a clear fire, and when ignited, transferred to the iron, and fresh fuel added. The iron was then put in a draught to heat up, or bellows were used, and the heat could be regulated by means of a little opening at the back.

And when all was well ironed and neatly folded up, it was aired in the old brick-oven after a bake, and the linen stored in a chest of drawers or coffer, laid up with lavender, rosemary, southernwood or balm. But as for the flannels and blankets, so susceptible to moth, these were sometimes put away with little bags tucked in their folds, containing old mens' clay-pipes ground up. A wonderfully effective anti-moth device.

As time passed, sundry labour-saving devices appeared, such as the Washing-Machine which was shown at the International Exhibition of 1862. This has a rocker base, and the washing was rocked against corrugated leaves by means of a bar handle (*Fig.* 17).

'Mangling Done Here' was a common sign to be seen in the windows of the houses of the poorer London streets, as also women and children taking home the washing in neat little parcels or covered baskets, evidence of thrift on the part of a poor working woman in an effort to enlarge the family budget. All this has entirely vanished.

Mangling Boards were in use prior to any mechanical contrivances. The clothes were wound round a small roller like a rolling-pin and these boards were rolled over by hand pressure. Many of them are of the nature of Love Tokens as the centre one shown in Figure 18. This is Dutch, dated 1636, was made for Annitien Pieters, and is most beautifully carved with hearts and arrows.

FIVE

THE DAIRY

FIFTY years ago butter-making was one of the arts or mysteries of farm life, the peculiar pride of the mistress. It was carried out once a week, preferably on a Tuesday, and does not seem to have caused quite such an upheaval as brewing or the monthly wash. Neither does it appear to have necessitated such early rising, but was accomplished during the morning between breakfast and the mid-day meal.

Old dairies sometimes exhibit a sign above the door or window thus: 'Dairy', 'Cheese Room', which is a reminder of the Window Tax Notice of the Act of Parliament, passed June 1st, 1808, but repealed July 24th, 1851. This imposed a tax of a certain scale on all windows of a dwelling house, but section 13 exempted windows of the above category, provided such rooms were used for that purpose and were not slept in or inhabited. Provided also that no glazing was used, but such windows were enclosed by lattice work, and notices in Roman lettering posted above.

The dairy attached to the farm-house was usually a one-storeyed building, and lay on the north or cool side of the house. It had a stone-flagged or brick floor, lattice windows, and an elder tree in attendance to ward off flies and evil spirits. Wide shelves running along the walls held the flat shallow pans into which the milk was emptied after each milking, and in which it was left for some hours to allow the cream to rise to the surface. It is said that more cream was obtained from pans of rough glazed pot earth than from the tin variety. The temperature of the dairy could be regulated by means of the lattice windows, which were provided with shutters that were moved according to the direction of the wind. Needless to say, the dairy was kept spotlessly clean.

The milk-pans or bowls were tended daily, and the cream was skimmed off by means of skimmers or fleeters (the latter term is from Suffolk), flattish round utensils, perforated, with a wooden handle. These were usually of tin but might be of brass or copper. First the index finger was run round the edge of the cream to detach it from the bowl, and then the cream was skimmed into a pail. To preserve the cream, some of which was a week old, it was necessary to stir it occasionally with flat wooden sticks known as cream-pot stirrers, ladles, or mungles in Hereford, and saltpetre was added. The skimmed milk was sold at three or four pints for a penny, or emptied into the swill-tubs for the pigs.

The dairy utensils were nearly all of wood, and were kept shiningly white by means of constant scourings. To this end wood-ash was used, and it was applied by wheat or rye straw wisps that were wetted and dipped into the ash.

When the churn was prepared, the interior had to be of a certain temperature. In more modern times this was gauged by a thermometer, but the older generation could tell by simply thrusting a hand into the churn. In cold weather the churn was rinsed out with hot water. The cream was then poured in, the opening closed, and the fun commenced:

Slow rolls the churn, its load of clogging cream
At once forgoes its quality and name;

From knotty particles first floating wide
Congealing butter's dash'd from side to side.

Butter is not made, it 'comes', as indicated by the
little verse that was often chanted while the churn
revolved:

> Come, butter, come.
> Peter stands at the gate,
> Waiting for a buttered cake,
> Come, butter, come.

Sometimes it came, sometimes it did not. And if it
came too soon it was flaccid and soft. The normal time
was 30 to 45 minutes. But it was possible to go on all
day and for the butter still not to come. When this
happened the cream was taken out, left all night and a
fresh start made in the morning. Once the operator had
begun she had to keep on, except for an occasional halt
to vent the churn and let out the air. If this was not done
the contents would *bloom*, or be covered with froth. But
she could tell by the rhythmical sound if all was well.
'Lump-lump . . . Lump-lump'; but should it be 'Lump
. . . lump', or 'Lump . . . lump', then trouble was in
store.

Owing to its capricious nature, butter was an easy
prey to spells and charms. Should an old witch put her
head in at the doorway while the process was in hand
and be unkindly treated, then good-bye butter! I heard
of a gipsy woman who appeared when the licensee of an
inn, to which a farm was attached, was busy churning for
his wife. Being somewhat nettled that morning he
grumpily bade the wanderer begone, whereupon she
informed him he would get no butter that day. Neither

did he! But an old shoe tied to the churn has been known to set things right.

When the butter arrived, the butter-milk was first let out of the churn, and the butter extracted by hand and placed in a butter keeler, a low tub on legs, in which was clean water. It was then worked to extract any more butter-milk, and washed with several applications of fresh water, the old water being let out by means of a waste-hole in the bottom of the keeler, bunged by a wooden peg. This done, the butter was placed on the wooden counter, and duly weighed up into pounds and half-pounds on old wooden scales.

Alternatively, it was sold in yards or pints (a pint is a little more than a pound, about 19 ounces). The pounds and half-pounds were patted up into brick shapes with butter-boards or pats, which were also known as Scotch-hands. These pats were sometimes ribbed, the finishing touches being given by a little ribbed roller, or by a butter marker which imprinted a pattern. These and similar dainty little designs so characteristic of more picturesque days are thought to have denoted the type of farm that produced the butter—a sheaf of corn indicating a mixed farm; sprigs of sweet-gale, a mountain pasture; a swan, a valley farm; a cow, some specially fine animal and a great milker. When the finishing touches had been applied the butter was left for the night so as to be ready for the morning.

A barrel-churn produced 46 pounds of butter in one operation, and was fitted inside with leaves or planes against which the cream flopped in the revolutions. The box of the churn illustrated in Figure 21 is of elm with nicely turned paterae on the two sides, but the paddles or fans are of box-wood or hickory to withstand the wear in the churning. Bearings for the iron shaft of the handle are formed by sections cut from leg-of-mutton bones. The sides are concave at the base to obviate any awkward right-angles within. It dates from the latter part of the eighteenth century or early in the nineteenth century, is much worm-eaten and was in use until a few months ago.

The reputation of the farmer's wife lay as much in her cheese as in her butter, although the latter ranked first. Cheese making was all part and parcel of dairy work, and was catered for by that portion of the dairy which was walled off by lattice work and formed the cheese room. This had to be maintained at a temperature of 65 degrees to 70 degrees allowing a little draught, though not enough dry air to crack the cheese. It was a seven-day week job, and has been described as a drudgery; certainly cheese making required more attention than butter, since the latter was a weekly affair, while each day called for some attention to cheeses. But drudgery was not in the dairy-maid's vocabulary, and all these things were taken in the daily stride. Before milk was sold to distant purchasers in bulk, it was made into cheese and butter, but so soon as transport facilities enabled the milk to be sent away, then this form of dairy work ceased on the farm.

Cleanliness was the first essential in cheese making, and all utensils had to be washed, first in cold water and then in hot. The water used had to be as pure as possible, and the pasturage free from strong smelling herbs such as garlic. All the same, vessels served more than one purpose, and often the copper that availed for washing and brewing days did duty also for heating the milk. Likewise the washing-tub, brewing or butter keeler became a cheese-tub as well. It was all hand labour, primitive yet effective, with temperatures gauged by instinct rather than thermometers.

The processes for cheese making varied with the kinds produced, and were traditional to the area and the genius of the locality, so that almost each county contributed its own special cheese made to ancient recipes. Of these many varieties Cheddar seems to have towered above all the others, and found many smaller varieties calling themselves by this great name. Of other notables there were Single and Double Gloucesters, Caerphilly, Dorset Blue or Blue Vinny, North Wilts Cheese, to mention some of the West of England varieties. These were essentially English, but a foreign influence crept in here and there, as in the Ewes' Milk Cheese which developed into the Wensleydale cheese. This was first made by Cistercian monks, who brought the craft from the Continent, at a small religious community established at Wensleydale, that was later to grow into Jervaulx Abbey. At the dissolution the secret became known to the owner of the nearby Cover Bridge inn, and from thenceforward was called Cover Bridge Cheese, later changing to Wensleydale.

And also the famous Parmesan, made from skimmed milk, from Parma in Italy. Curiously enough this was a man's job, as it required strength to handle the curd, slipping it into a large cloth while still in the kettle and transferring it to a mould without a bottom. This had to be done with speed as the cheese hardened so rapidly.

It should be mentioned this cheese was made in a large copper kettle suspended over the fire by means of a crane. The milk was stirred until it reached 125 degrees Fahrenheit, then the kettle was turned from the fire. When bubbling ceased, rennet tied in a linen bag was added and squeezed several times over the surface. The rennet was then taken out, and the milk left until the curd formed, normally three-quarters-of-an-hour. The kettle was returned to the fire and heated to 150 degrees, being well stirred, and the curd divided while heating. A quarter of the whey was then taken out, and the curd heated to 180 degrees, being well stirred all the time, and a few pinches of powdered saffron added. When finished, salted and covered with linseed oil, it was something to write about: 'There's no hope of recovery of that Welsh madman; was undone by a mouse that spoiled him a parmesant; lost his wits for 't.' Middleton, *Changeling*, i. 2.

In many recipes the evening milk seems to figure most, but morning milk was also used as noted in the extract from a Household Book of Hengrave Hall, Suffolk:

'The remainte of household provysions, 1607. Cheeses of the last remaynt at the hall dairie, XX made there this q^{rt}: of ordinary cheese, iiij^{xx}, iij-morning milk cheese, X: received in presents of morning milk cheeses, iiij: Cheeses of the last remaynte at the grange dairie, cxlvj: made there this q^{rt} ccxxxiij: cheeses of the last remaynte at Chevington dairie, c.lxv: made there this q^{rt}—of ordinary cheeses, ccx—and of morning milk cheeses, viij—wherof spent in house at the hall, lxxvij—spent at the grange, clij—spent at Chevington, xxiij—sold xliij—sent to the Lo. Cooke at assise time of morning milk cheeses, ij—given of ordinary cheeses iiij.'

Generally speaking the evening milk was run into the cheese-tub, or on to leads, and the cream which had risen on this in the morning was skimmed off (fleeted in Suffolk), and used for butter. Then the morning milk, still warm, was added to the skimmed evening milk. In some cases the cream of the evening's milk was returned

to it, after the milk had been brought to the right heat
for renneting. Sometimes the whole of the milk was
heated, otherwise part only sufficed to bring the
remainder to the required temperature, which varied
according to the seasons, and the nature of the pasturage.
For example, milk produced on a chalky soil was raised
68 degrees to 72 degrees in summer, and from 72 degrees
to 78 degrees in spring and autumn. Clay called for a
higher temperature—74 degrees to 78 degrees in summer,
and 78 degrees to 84 degrees in colder weather.

The milk was curdled by means of rennet, made from
vells soaked in whey, sometimes flavoured with sweet
herbs. This took an hour to coagulate. The resultant
curd was then broken, which might be done by hand,
stirring-stick, shovel-breaker, American curd knife or
curd breaker. Hereford Museum possesses some of these
latter which consist of spiked wooden rollers, operated
much like the old beet-cutting machines. Another form
was a cutter similar to that used for removing the ails
or avils of barley, but lighter in make. Care had to be
taken in this process lest the curd was broken too fine,
or bruised, which might result in a white whey and loss
of fat. Neither must it be stirred for more than a few
minutes after the breaking, lest the cheese became dry
and hard.

The broken curd was then allowed to settle in the
tub, and develop sufficient acidity to shrink from the tub
sides so that the hand could be inserted in the gap. The
whey was then drawn off and the curds piled up in the
tub and left to drain for an hour. Salt was now added,
half-ounce to each one-pound curd. It was then transferred to the vats.

These vats (*Fig.* 20) are interesting survivals today, cut
from the solid, elm, oak or beech, varying in diameter

from 9 inches to 16 inches, with a depth of some 3 inches, bound with metal. Sometimes cloths were used, but often not. The vats were placed one atop the other, left for a while to drain through the holes pierced in the base, before being placed in the cheese press where they remained for twenty-four hours before being turned. They were finally placed on the shelves of the cheese room to mature.

The old cheese presses (*Fig.* 22), of which many survive, were sometimes of wood weighted with iron or stone weights, but often composed of a block of stone weighing 5 to 6 hundredweights, fitted to a frame. To the top of the stone a stout rope was fixed by a staple, which was run through an overhead pulley and connected to a small windlass, the raising and lowering process being effected by hand-spikes.

Suffolk 'Bang' was a hard cheese, made with skimmed milk, and was often eaten with fat pork, making a staying meal. The cheese was set in front of the fire, and as it softened was scraped off and smeared over the pork. 'Trip', on the other hand, was a small cheese made in summer to be eaten in its soft and curdy state. Otherwise it soon became dry, tough and uneatable.

Suffolk Stilton was a large cheese made with new milk, to which was added suet to cause mould. These Stiltons were often placed under the tap of a cask of old beer or wine, the drip from which assisted in the ripening.

Fuller in his *Worthies* has a good deal to say about the various county cheeses, but awards the palm to Wales: 'Foxes are said to be the best tasters of the finest flesh, flies of the sweetest grapes, and mice of the tenderest cheese: and the last (when they could compass choice in that time) have given their verdict for the goodness of the Welsh.'

Among valuable presents made to Henry VIII in 1533 by his courtiers, were 'a box with flowers of needlework and six Suffolk cheeses' from Lady Calthrop, and 'treacle and a cheese of Parmason' from Anthony Cassydony. These appear in a list which includes: 'a gold ball for perfume', 'a dog-book of fine gold', and 'a tablet of gold with a device of Adam and Eve'.

Cheeses were sold in great quantities at the various country Fairs, and purchasers would buy a year's supply at a time, sending them home in their wagons.

SIX

THE DOMESTIC PIG

Here lies John Higgs
A famous man for killing pigs,
For killing pigs was his delight
Both morning, afternoon and night.

GLOUCESTERSHIRE EPITAPH

THE story of the pig is long and fascinating, since it is as old as husbandry and almost world wide. Besides having provided delectable dishes for the table, the pig has inspired an unequalled page in our literature: 'I speak not of your grown porkers—things between pig and pork—those hobbydehoys—but a young and tender suckling—under a moon old—guiltless as yet of the sty—with no original speck of the *amor immunditiae*, the hereditary failing of the first parent, yet manifest—his voice as yet not broken, but something between a childish treble and a grumble—the mild forerunner or *praeludium* of a grunt.'

'*He must be roasted*. I am not ignorant that our ancestors ate them seethed or boiled—but what a sacrifice of the exterior tegument!'

Or as Ben Jonson has it in *Bartholomew Fair:* 'Now pig is a meat, and a meat that is nourishing and may be longed for, and so consequently eaten; it may be eaten; very exceedingly well eaten.'

Besides which it figures in Holy Writ, in that most human of all stories: 'The Prodigal Son', and in that episode, but faintly understood by Western minds, of the

'Gadarene Swine'. In which one's sympathies are apt to go out to the unoffending pigs.

How great its influence has been is seen even in our nomenclature such as the Hog's Back, and in archaeology in the 'Swine-penny', coins unearthed in its rootling activities. While it called into being one of our old-time parish officers—the Hog-Reeve or Hog-Constable. Naturally it figures in folk-lore, for pigs are credited with being able to see the wind. 'Swine being seen to carry bottles of hay or straw to any place and hide them', is an omen of rain. In marriages of long ago: 'The bryde anonyted the poostes of the doores with swyne's grease, because she thought by that meanes to dryve awaye all misfortune, whereof she had her name in Latin, *Uxor ab ungendo*.' And who does not know of the Boar's Head at Christmas? 'Payed for iij sheets thick grose paper to decke the bores heade in Christmas xijd.'

'More payd to Bushe of Bury, paynter, for paynting the bores heade with sondry colors, ijs.'

Pannage, or the right of pasturing swine in woods, figures large in old documents, as the swine-herd in ancient chronicles. But just as these wart hogs fed on the mast of beech and acorns, or as Chaucer remarks: 'They eten mast, hawes, and swych pownage,' so also they had a nose for that delectable fungus, the truffle, now hardly known. In the South of France pigs were used to hunt these, but here a little dog was trained to pursue the quest.

An old country maxim, long prevalent, was that a pig must be killed in the waxing of a moon rather than the waning, so that its flesh did not shrink in the cooking. Which idea was founded in far off days, as this, dated 1664: 'Kill swine in or near the full of the Moon and the flesh will the better prove in boiling.'

Almost every county in England has produced its own breed of pigs, and we have amongst others, Large and Middle White, Tamworth, Berkshire, Essex Black, and the Lincolnshire Curly-Coated. All of which bear shining records in the Royal Agricultural Society of England, besides those of local moment.

Much of country life, and indeed cottage economy generally centred about the pig, since most cottagers aspired to the rearing of one or two in a sty at the end of their garden, although often that hovel was all too near the house. For as Mr. Cobbett remarked: 'They are great softeners of the temper, and promoters of the domestic harmony.' To this end all the kitchen waste went into the swill-tub, care having been taken that no soda was used in the cooking, so that any surplus food, and the water used in cooking could be emptied into this tub.

Killing the pig was a great event in the domestic round, full of the greatest satisfaction to all concerned, save the pig. News of such an intention was often voiced abroad, and if the hour permitted, the children would join in and watch the sacrifice. How much of fun and frolic was inherent in this can be gathered from the rhyme sometimes chanted on St. Valentine's day:

> Good Morrow, Valentine!
> How it do hail:
> When father's pig die
> You shall ha' its tail.

> Good Morrow, Valentine!
> How thundering hot:
> When father's pig die
> You shall ha' its jot.

The jot, it may be explained, is the extremity near the tail, from which the finest of the black puddings were made.

Farmhouses, presumably, had sufficient staff to deal with their own killing, but in the case of the cottage itinerant pig-killers or spare-time butchers, perchance the village postman, went about killing and cutting-up pigs for a shilling or one-and-sixpence a piece. The carcase was placed on the stool, legs hanging down on either side, and the head was cut off first followed by the legs. A chalk-line was then used to mark two lines down the back by the spine, along which the butcher cut to take out the chine. These chines when properly cured were delicious eating. The butchers carried their tools on their back in an old flail basket made of plaited rush, as shown in Figure 23. These tools (also shown) would consist of knives, scrapers or scuds fashioned from an old scythe blade, a nail extractor, and gambrels or buckers which were inserted between the hind legs when hanging up the carcase. Of these latter it is interesting to recall the old Suffolk riddle:

As straight as a maypole,
As little as a pin,
As bent as a bucker,
And as round as a ring.

In some instances a permanent fixture of the garden was the pig-pole, from which, gibbet-like, the carcase hung.

Amid much lamentation and wailing, the pig was removed from the sty and 'stuck'. When dead, straw would be heaped about the body and ignited to burn off the long hairs, then the carcase was placed on the hog-stool, as described above. These stools formed part of the equipment of most houses, and took their place with the brewing utensils, so that those without, and poorer neighbours could borrow. They were about five feet long, and some eighteen inches from the ground, supported on splayed legs, of ash, elm or oak. I have a more elaborate specimen, fitted with a circular lead dish at one end, with drainage pipe to run off the blood.

Next the carcase was scalded, and scraped to remove any remaining hairs. It was then hung up and cut down the middle from snout to tail, and the entrails removed. These consisted of the pluck (liver), lights, milt and veil. The carcase was duly divided into loin, and belly or spring, fore-legs or hands, back-legs or hams, and the chaps, which were the two halves of the face.

The entrails, to which were added tongue, heart, feet, eye-bones, and rinds off the back, were all boiled up and turned into pork-cheeses; while the blood and other offal made black puddings and faggots. Brawn was made from the pig's head. (Bores of the last remaynte xj—whereof killed at the hall for brawne, j). Lard was derived from any of the fat which could be melted down, and leaf-lard came from the back. This was not only a great adjunct in cooking, producing lovely pastry, but was often used instead of butter, flavoured with rosemary. The scraps, crisp and dainty fragments left from the trying down of the lard were a great delicacy, which still linger fragrantly in the memories of the older folk. Particularly the scrap-pies, made of scraps mixed with currants and baked in pie-plates. The covererings of the intestines were cleaned and used for sausage skins, so that literally nothing of the pig was wasted.

Pork sausages—those delectable country morsels, now only a memory—were all of meat, seasoned with sage, black pepper and nutmeg. They were hand-made, the

meat chopped up on a chopping board, which latter
was either a board framed on three sides by a fillet of
wood, or a box. The chopper was as shown in Figure 24,
or it might be shaped like a garden hoe of the straight
variety with a short handle. The skins were gathered on
to the shank of the little tin funnel, and the meat pushed
through the hopper by the two thumbs. Eight sausages
went to a pound.

Apart from the necessity of this hand-work, since there
were no mincing machines, there was virtue in it, as it
retained some of the juices in the meat that were squeezed
out and lost by the machine. Queen Victoria noted this
and insisted that her sausages should be made by hand,
to her own recipe, which included eggs.

Pork-pies, another dainty, suggest a local habitation
and a name, fragrant by reason of recipes long grown
old. When sliced, presenting a galantine of picturesque
and flavoursome appearance, with whole eggs shining
like harvest moons in a meaty sky. And did not the very
shape of these pies with their brown pastry covers give
rise to the model for a hat favoured by our Victorian
ancestors?

Hams were cured and pickled at home, a laboursome
process but one of love. Pickle was prepared and poured
into a ham-pan of red earthenware (*Fig.* 25), the ham
laid in this, and daily turned and rubbed all over with the
liquid. It was then branded and sent to the drier,
who was often the cooper, since it was his oak chippings
that provided the smoke most efficacious in the process.
And here is an excellent recipe for Sweet Pickle, which
hails from Suffolk: 'Take 1 lb. coarse salt, 1 lb. brown
sugar, 1 pint of old beer, ½ oz. prunella (broken up),
1 lb. brown treacle, 2 pints of cold water.'

On its return from drying, it was sewn up in a muslin

bag, care having been taken to rub salt into the nose and close to the bone; it was then hung up until required. This curing took place from October 11th (old Michaelmas), to March 11th.

White salt bacon, taken off the flank of a large fat pig, also known as flick pork, was salted in a tub, or pork-pot of red earthenware. It was usually held under the brine by means of a large stone taken out of the fields. When cooked, it was first boiled, the rind scored, and then put in the oven and baked for about a quarter of an hour to make it crisp.

J. Alfred Eggars in his *Remembrances* tells a good story. It concerned a lady who took great interest in her estate and was greatly loved by all the tenants. She always occupied the chair at her Audit Dinner, and on one of these occasions the oldest of those present was asked to propose her health. On rising to his feet he was so overcome that he was at a loss what to say. He began: 'Well, ma'am, you are like a good fat hog!'

'Really, Mr. ——, what do you mean?'

'Well, ma'am, what I means is, every bit of you is good!'

SEVEN

LIGHTING AND HEATING

When you go to get a lite,
Ye flint agen ye stele you strike.
Have match & good tinder dry,
Snick & then ye fire will fly.

THE problem of artificial lighting must have been very acute, so much so that the only effective means of tackling it must have been to ignore it and go to bed with the sun. How dim were the lights when the earliest form of lighting became available can only be realised by concentrated effort. And yet the fine work accomplished by candle-light, even rushlight, has to be seen to be believed. This too, by eyes unaided by glasses, which can be partly explained by absence of glare in the lighting, and longer life in the natural eyesight as a consequence. Firelight must have been greater than most lamps, and its comfortable glow suggests the best in the English home.

A floating wick in oil provided the earliest lamp, but in the English countryside the rushlight was the general illuminant for many a century. This was made from peeled rushes steeped in fat and were known in Suffolk as fried straws or sleepers. These when lighted would burn an hour, but needed constant adjustment in the holder, a service often performed by a junior member of the society. The classic description of these lights was given by Gilbert White in his *Selbourne*, thus: 'The proper species of rush for this purpose seems to be the *juncus conglomeratus*, or common soft rush, which is to be found in most moist pastures, by the sides of streams, and under hedges. These rushes are in best condition in the height of summer; but may be gathered, so as to serve the purpose well, quite on to autumn. It would be needless to say, that the largest and longest are best. Decayed labourers, women and children, make it their business to procure and prepare them. As soon as they are cut, they must be flung into water, and kept there; for otherwise they will dry and shrink, and the peel will not run. At first, a person would find it no easy matter to divest a rush of its peel, or rind, so as to leave one regular, narrow, even rib, from top to bottom, that may support the pith; but this, like other feats, soon becomes familiar, even to children; and we have seen an old woman, stone blind performing this business with great despatch, and seldom failing to strip them with the nicest regularity. When these *junci* are thus far prepared, they must lie out on the grass to be bleached, and take the dew for some nights, and afterwards be dried in the sun.

'Some address is required in dipping these rushes in the scalding fat, or grease; but this knack also is to be attained by practice. The careful wife of an industrious Hampshire labourer obtains all her fat for nothing, for she saves the scummings of her bacon pot for this use; and, if the grease abounds with salt, she causes the salt to be precipitated to the bottom, by setting the scummings in a warm oven. Where hogs are not much in use, and especially by the sea-side, the coarser animal oils will come very cheap. A pound of common grease may be procured for fourpence; and about six pounds of grease will dip a pound of rushes; and one pound of rushes may be bought for a shilling; so that a pound of rushes, medicated and ready for use, will cost three shillings. If men that keep bees will mix a little wax with the grease, it will give it consistency, and render it more cleanly, and make the rushes burn longer: mutton suet would have the same effect.

'A good rush which measures in length two feet four inches and a half, being minuted, burnt only three minutes short of an hour; and a rush of still greater length has been known to burn one hour and a quarter.

'These rushes give a good, clear light. Watchlights (coated with tallow), it is true, shed a dismal one—"darkness visible"—but then the wicks of these have two ribs of the rind, or peel, to support the pith, while the wick of the peeled rush has but one. The two ribs are intended to impede the progress of the flame, and make the candle last.

'An experienced old housekeeper assures me, that one pound and a half of rushes completely supplied his family the year round since working people burn no candle in the long days, because they rise and go to bed by daylight.'

Candles ran parallel with rush-lights and finally superseded them. They were made either as dips or in moulds. If the former the wick was often of rush, and they were dipped repeatedly in fat, giving them several thicknesses until they assumed candle form. The latter were made by placing wicks—later specially home-knitted and dipped in boracic to obviate the snaast that would develop as the candle burnt—inside the mould, and then pouring in the fat, the candle being made point downwards as they are today in the most elaborate and modern methods. Candle-moulds (*Fig.* 31) were an adjunct of every well-ordered kitchen. The dips were tied together in pound bunches by the wicks, and were known as Twelves,

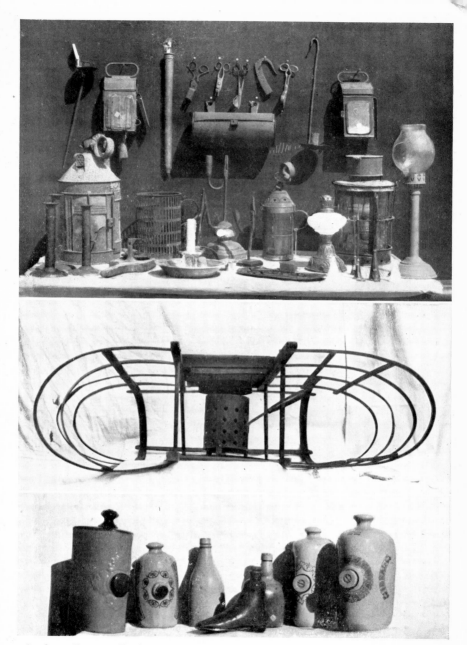

26. *above:* Pew candlestick, carriage candle-lamp, candle mould, snuffers, wick lifter, wick scissors, flint-strike, snuffers, candle box below, hanging candle holder, carriage lamp. *below back:* Horn lantern, wind-proof candlestick, rushlight holders, lantern made from bottle by gypsy, oil lamp, oil lantern, candle lamp. *front:* 18th cent. adjustable candlesticks, workshop candlestick, Sheffield plate candlestick, snuffers in tray, extinguishers. **27.** Sussex bed-warmer. **28.** Hot water bottles.

LIGHTING AND HEATING

29. Early fire-engine, hand manual type. **30.** Footstool with container for hot water, ginger beer bottle used as child's hot water bottle, muff in tin box holder. **31.** Candle mould, evidently for making twelve candles to the pound (known as 'twelveses'. **32.)** Warming pans.

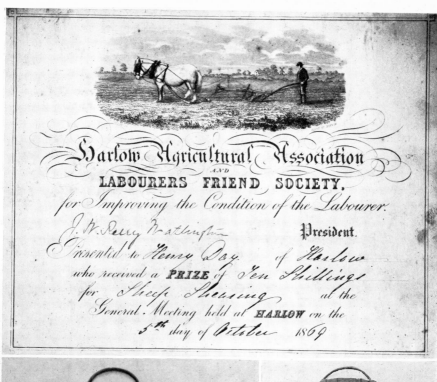

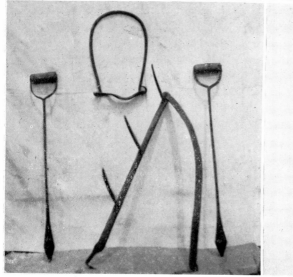

33. Certificate awarded to a boy of fifteen for shearing a sheep at a County Show. **34.** Dabs, dibs, debs or dibbling irons (Rockets = a row of holes made by dibbling), cow yoke (above), wooden scythe bail. **35.** Harvest bottles, costrels or firkins.

BYGONES OF FIELD AND FARM

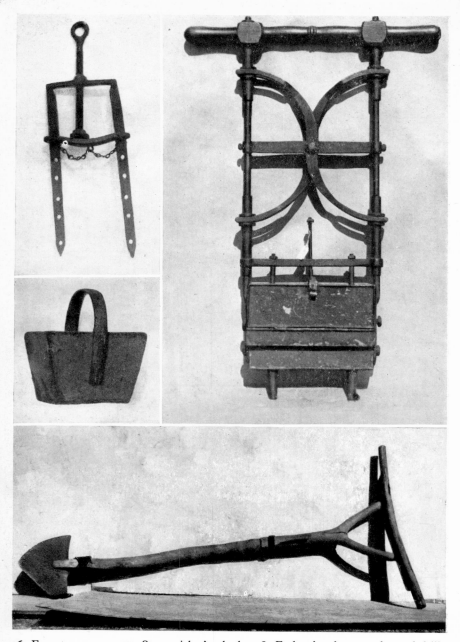

36. Faggot cramp. **37.** Stone-picker's hod. **38.** Early hand-operated seed-drill.
39. Breast-plough.

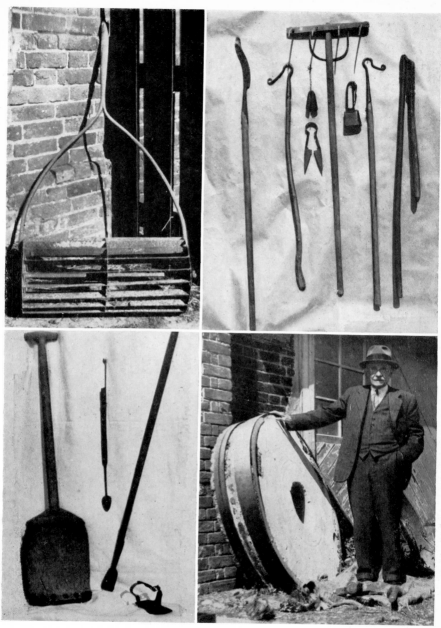

40. Barley hummeller.   **41.** Pea make (any crop that is severed from the soil and left to dry is said to be 'made' when it is in a fit state to be carried), shepherd's crook, cow bell, sheep shears, bean rake, sheep bell (canister type), crook, and flail.   **42.** Mud scuppit, rat-poisoner's spoon, dock spud, digging shoe.   **43.** The miller stands by his stones.

44. Flour boulter. 45. Post mill in full working order at Saxtead, Suffolk. 46. Miller's scales. 47. Miller's scales: underside of chair, showing scoopings out.

THE MILLER AND [HIS MILL

48. *standing at back:* Bill hook, flagging iron, driver; *left:* (from back to front) Part of swift, another, dowelling stock and bit. *centre:* Buzz, hollowing knife, swift. *right:* Part of swift, another, hollow knife, part of swift. (The various parts of swifts were made by the cooper as spares). 49. Cooper's adze, reamer, topping plane. 50. Cooper's side axe. 51. Coopered bucket, two butter cups and prints, pestle and spirit cask. *back:* Potato smasher or life preserver, flour scoop, pastry stamp.

THE COOPER

52. Foot power loom, preserved in Lavenham Church, Suffolk. **53.** Spinning wheel of English walnut with ivory enrichments. **54.** Wool combs. **55.** Spinning wheel or bobbin winder.

HOME SPUN AND WOVEN

Long Nines or Short Sixteens to the pound. They were
hung up on nails and cut off as required. Tallow-candles,
also in bunches, were a characteristic of country shops.
Special candles were made for carriage lamps, and some
with two wicks called Moons, were used at sea.

Three types or grades of candles emerged, tallow,
beeswax and composite, and it was by the aid of the two
latter that grandmother executed her bewildering and
fine stitch. Although candles were cheap according to
our standards (a farthing candle was known as a Long
Lady), yet their consumption must have added considerably to the family exchequer. An insight on this is
gained from *Nollekens and his Times*, where the parsimony
of the old sculptor is well brought out: 'Candles were
never lighted at the commencement of the evening, and
whenever they heard a knock at the door, they would
wait until they heard a second ring, lest the first should
have been a runaway, and their candle wasted. Mr. and
Mrs. Nollekens used a flat candlestick when there was
anything to be done; and I have been assured that a pair
of moulds, by being well nursed, and put out when
company went away, once lasted them a whole year!'
'By Candle Light', is suggestive of softness, quiet and a
serene peace; while the guttering candle has symbolised
the passing of the days.

Candle-making was for long a craft, and out of it came
the Tallow and Wax Chandlers' Guilds, with great
privileges attaching to them. On the other hand it was a
domestic craft, and in Wales women went about making
candles at houses where the fat and wicks were supplied,
in the same way as others went to do the washing or the
brewing. (For V days work in making candle at vid.
the day, ijs. vjd. *Household Book* of Hengrave Hall, 1572.)
There were also certain great occasions centring about

5

this form of light. The Pascal Candle was a huge post-like affair of wax, specially made for burning in churches at that season. Candles acted as time-pieces from very early times, notably when King Alfred (871–901), ordered the making of time-keeping candles. These were of the courtly beeswax, and six cost as much as 72 pence. Each had twelve inches marked on it, and when the six were lit in succession they burned for 24 hours. Auctions were held by 'Inch of Candle'. It was lighted to start the bidding and the winner was he who made the last bid ere it flickered out.

A whole armoury of appliances for holding the rush-lights and candles came into use, mostly blacksmith-made, and indeed a whole range of lanterns, first horn and later with glass sides. The wire lantern is of interest in that a lighted candle could be carried across a wind-swept yard without the flame being blown out. Candles also required snuffers, many of which are beautifully wrought, now constituting excellent ornaments, complete with their tray. Extinguishers, that now look like clown's caps were necessary to prevent smell when the light was put out (*Fig.* 26).

The first oil lamps to appear were the Moderators which burnt colza oil, and were invented in 1836. There was a spring inside which was wound up by a key, and this forced the oil to the top of a round wick; the surplus oil could be seen dripping back into the reservoir. This lamp required winding every hour or so, and very careful trimming but it gave a nice soft light. Another was the Wanzer lamp for burning paraffin, patent number 2833, dated 1887. It has a clockwork-driven fan in the base, wound up by a key. This worked for six hours at a stretch, and caused a draught of air to pass up the centre, producing a white light. No chimney or globe was required.

The paraffin lamp did not arrive until about 1870, with at first single, flat wicks, then duplex, followed by the circular type. They soon ousted the Moderator and dispensed with candles as means of general lighting, as they are being ousted today by electricity. Candles, however, as a bedroom illuminant and a portable light, continued until the beginning of this century, and all great country houses provided each guest with a candle in a stick to light them to bed. These were arranged in the hall at the appropriate time.

All these appliances were the bane of the housemaid. Lamps required trimming, not an easy task, and for this wick-scissors appeared on the market, shaped much like snuffers, but not to be confused with them. The glasses were awkward to clean, and if the wicks were not even fishtails appeared on them, or the room might be covered with smuts. Lamp-black was of the cimmerian depths, and was black indeed.

Ignition was first gained by tinder, flint and steel, and the old tinder-boxes, usually round, often fitted with a candle-socket in the lid, now form interesting museum pieces. This old custom and method became so endemic to our economy that I have heard a woman exclaim on washing a sheet become very thin in wear as being 'only fit for tinder'. Besides old cloth, tinder was provided from touchwood or punk, which was wood decayed by a fungal attack. A more advanced form was the flint-lock tinder pistol, operated like a small firearm by the pulling of a trigger. The flint in striking threw a spark on the tinder which was held in a small pan. Later came the matches, first sulphur-tipped that could not be struck, but were ignited from the burning tinder. Various wax vestas and safety matches appeared later and are with us today. The smoker was catered for by fusees and other

long-burning stinks, some of which claimed to light a
pipe or a cigar even in a wind. Spills were an adjunct to
most cottage mantelpieces, made of folded paper. They
were of ancient foundation, since they called forth sundry
little vases for their accommodation. At one time there
was an inmate of the Workhouse at Cuckfield, Sussex,
who could light his pipe by the aid of a knife, a flint
picked up in the fields, and a tuft of thistledown.

Heating must have been a problem, considering how
cold houses and cottages must have been any distance
from the fire. Charcoal, however, solved something of
this problem as it could burn in a brazier in the centre
of an apartment without a flue, although care had to be
taken of the fumes. This is well illustrated by the braziers
of wrought-iron, on tripod stand, mounted on castors,
with perforated lid. A pair of these are preserved in
Barking Church, Suffolk, and others are to be found in
the Colleges of Oxford. This fuel burnt clearly, gave
forth a great heat, and could be stimulated in its consumption by means of bellows.

Most villagers had Common Rights which might
include the cutting of turves, flaggs or peat. When these
were cut professionally for resale, three implements
were required, the peat-spade for cleaning the top spit,
the knife for making the opening, and most important
of all, the becket for cutting. This tool was so shaped
that each piece of peat was cut to a uniform size. One
man cut the blocks or 'mumps', and another carried
them away to dry, being laid on their sides, or they were
made into cocks, or 'hiles'. They were then stacked into
pyramids, shoulder high and about five feet wide at the
bottom. Fires made from these were very difficult to
kindle and were seldom allowed to go out.

And, of course, no fireplace was complete without its

bellows; an ancient elemental device so necessary where the fuel is wood. The regard in which these were held is expressed in the inscription cut on one dated 1673:

Bellows like a quiat wife
Send out Breath and make no strife.

But they had other uses as noted in the conversation between two maids as recorded in the *Connoisseur* for 1911: 'Mary (to her fellow servant); "Oh dear! I dont know what's the matter with this kettle; it runs so slowly." Jane (from the North): "Wy gyurl, why dont you get the bellasses, and blaa doon the kettle spoot? A've seen me fether do it lots of times." ' Mechanical Blowers, ingenious and beautifully made, came later to supply a more fastidious and longer purse.

Warming the bed was indeed a ritual as it was a necessity considering the linen sheets that were often used. The commonest means of doing this was with a warming-pan, examples of which must have been found in every household, since they figure in old lists among the goods and chattels of those who were removed to institutions, or whose goods were sold under orders of poor-law officials. They were of various kind, of which the most common type was used for embers. Some have survived with a hollow tube-like handle; these were for charcoal and could be stirred to greater heat if one blew down the handle. Another type was for hot water, while yet others, smaller and fashioned like a square box, were used with heated salt. These may have been peculiar to the coast or to areas near salt-pans. Ember or brand tongs were used to put the glowing embers into the pans.

Bed-wagons were also used—huge open-work band-box-like contrivances amid which a charcoal brazier was placed (*Fig.* 27). They seem to have been peculiar to Sussex, and were made individually, since no two are alike; it is possible that they may have been fashioned by trug-makers. Probably they were used more particularly for airing rather than for heating beds; although a correspondent recently in *Country Life* stated that something of a similar character is still used in parts of Italy. He said that a bed so warmed was a delight to get into.

Hot bricks were a common form amongst poor people, who not only placed them in the bed wrapped up in red flannel (a protective colour), but sat with them in their laps. A few drops of turpentine on the flannel placed on the hot brick were efficacious in the case of lumbago and tic-douloureux. The oven plate was also taken to bed duly wrapped in flannel. And sheets of brown paper sewn between thin blankets, or placed inside the sleeved waistcoat were effective as an insulator. As for hot water bottles, one of those nice old stoneware beer bottles was sufficient for the elders, and the ginger beer variety served the children (*Fig.* 30).

Victorian times saw many inventions, one of which was the *Instra*, with the catchword 'Warmth is Life'. This was a fuel in packet form, held in a small perforated container that slowly smouldered, and the instructions for use read like an essay in grammar: 'To be warm, put inside pocket: to be warmer, hook up just behind and below the hip-bone underneath the coat; if very chill, hook up on one or other side of the back bone between the shoulder; for railway travelling get the anklet strap; to air a damp bed quickly, put a chair in bed and the *Instra* inside.' It was also used in the form of a bicycle handle.

Carriage Warmers holding hot water were numerous as they were various. There were others known as

Stomach Warmers, and quite small holders were provided for the muff and known as hand warmers. While it was possible to obtain a footstool with a hot water container inside.

In case of fire—that elemental fear in man—we might consider the old hand-manual fire engine that is preserved in the lovely church of Lavenham, Suffolk. It dates from 1725, and was one of the originals issued by the Insurance Societies, and a copy of the first made by Newsham. On this are two leather buckets, products of local saddlers (*Fig. 29*).

EIGHT

BYGONES OF FIELD AND FARM

Writing and Ploughing are two different talents.
JETHRO TULL

THE interest invoked by bygones of field and farm is very considerable. It is an interest born of wonder at the stamina inherent in those, our ancestors, who wielded these hand tools all the livelong day, toiling without the aid of machine, tirelessly producing the essentials of life. Think of the sower, walking hour after hour over heavy acres, casting the seed from his seed-lip, with rhythm and grace, transforming a daily task into a dignified and splendid progress. Or the mower wielding the scythe under a relentless sun, dawn to dusk, with a body swing that had about it the quality of music. And when they had done the day's toil, they walked their three or five miles home, as they had made that excursion before commencing the morning's labour, without so much as five minutes' grace. Which calls to mind the lament of an old land worker of nearly ninety, who could neither read nor write: 'I eddicated my children (eleven of them), but they not half as good as I. Waste their time reading the paaper. Can't do a day's work.'

For convenience we might take these bygones in the order of the farmer's year, with first ploughing, either by the breast-plough of ancient inception (push-plough in Westmorland), or various types of wooden ploughs, of which not many have survived to this day. Ploughs, like the other implements, took upon themselves local colour, as the old Norfolk and Suffolk Gallows Ploughs, one wheel in the furrow and one out, and the one-armed Charlies.

The Breast-Plough differed little in form from the shovel-shaped plough evolved by the Saxons, which cut a furrow slice of a kind, and was the first known attempt at ploughing. This breast-plough was made of steel or wrought iron, was flat except at the left side where it was turned up, and measured in some cases 15 inches in length and breadth, and in others some 12 inches by 9 inches. The point was known as the picket, and this, with the edges, and the cutting part of the turned-up side (known as the counter), were ground to a very keen edge, the stone for the purpose being carried to the field where the man worked (*Fig.* 39).

The beam or haft, was of wood, and was fixed to the socket on the face of the plough by wedges, these also served the purpose of raising or lowering the beam to suit the height of a man, the soil he had to deal with, and the depth he wished to go. In early days the beam was five to six feet long, later being reduced to four-feet-six inches. It was often forked where it joined the crutch or cross handle, some two feet wide, into which it was morticed. Usually the beam was straight, but in some cases slightly curved. The weight of the whole varied, but does not appear to have exceeded 40 pounds at most.

It was worked by pressure of the chest against the cross handle in a series of jerks. Later, the ploughman was furnished with a board slung round the waist; and later by two pieces of wood worn over the thighs, known as clappers. These were of beech, hollowed out to fit the front of the thighs. A leather loop was nailed to the upper part of these, and they were suspended from a leather belt worn loosely round the waist, the lower parts being fitted with straps that buckled round the legs above the knees. They appeared much as womens' stays, with hinges at the side.

Breast-Ploughs took skilful making and a careful choice of wood, while the iron tip required frequent renewal. Sometimes one pushed and another pulled by cords, while a third guided and turned. Hitting stones gave a nasty knock. Breast-ploughing has been described as 'the most slavish work in husbandry'.

Breast-ploughing did not do the work of the horse-plough, but merely cleansed the top soil and provided material for burnbaking, otherwise known as paring and burning; a practice largely carried out in the Cotswolds and the Chilterns. This entailed great hardship from exposure in bad weather as the fires required constant attention, often during the night. The resultant ash provided an excellent manure, no other being required, producing wonderful crops, particularly turnips.

Wooden ploughs often had a turn-furrow of beech and a beam of ash or elm. They were particularly good in heavy ground, slipping the dirt well and especially so in soft ground. An absence of wheels gave them less chance to clog, but they were apt to wear out quickly, and were of little use where there was gravel or stone. In some cases they were used with as many as six horses, but often they were drawn by oxen, which were slow but sure, and took a wide turn at the headlands.

Gertrude Jekyll writes thus of them—1900—'The old wooden plough is seldom seen now, though it lingers on one good old farm within reach, and is well liked by the men who work it. It is generally used with two coulters. . . . A forked stick lies along the left-hand stilt, the forked end resting in an iron loop on the inside of the thick end of the beam. It is for the ploughman to reach and hook away, without stopping his team, any roots or tough weedy rubbish that hangs up between the share and the coulters.'

After ploughing came rolling, first by the wooden rollers often made from a round oak tree set aside for the purpose. These old rollers wore up all too quickly, especially when carted along the roads from field to field, which was apt to take out the middle of them. I have known some of these survive as gate posts. Another form was the Kit-Kat roller, thicker in the middle than at the ends, which was used for flattening the sides of the furrows. Additional weight could be obtained by placing a log across the shafts. Other than rollers, clod-beaters were used, something like a beetle of wood, wielded by women and boys. They were nine to ten inches long, were made of elm or beech, and had a handle not quite so long as a pitchfork. The pay was eightpence a day, or four shillings a week.

Which brings us to sowing and drilling. J. A. Eggars in his *Remembrances* tells of the ancient Surrey custom of the head-carter at drilling with a team of four horses, before commencing would exclaim: 'Well, lads, are you all ready?' Then, taking off his hat: 'May God send us luck.' And an old man when he had finished sowing a field would take off his hat and say: 'With God's blessing may we have a crop.'

The earliest form of sowing was by the broadcast method, in which the sower walked from side to side of his land throwing the seed, first right then left, with a rhythmic grace. This can often be seen today in the sow-ing of artificial manures, but is seldom resorted to for seed, owing to the uneveness of distribution. Drilling was the term given to the sowing of beans and peas in channels, or furrows by hand, and the earliest form of this must have been by the old dibbling irons, also known as dibs, dabs or debs. In this case the operator walked backwards, an iron in each hand, to which he gave a deft twist of the wrist, making a slight indentation in the soil to right and left of his path. This row of holes the whole length of the stetch was known as a rocket. He was followed by women and children, known as droppers, who, with equal dexterity, dropped the seeds into the holes by a deft jerking of the thumb over the face of the forefinger. As there was a song for most things in those days, they often chanted:

> Four seeds in a hole;
> One for the rook, one for the crow,
> One to rot, and one to grow.

These irons were designed for corn or beans, the latter having a larger knop at the end. Dibbled wheat was said to grow finer than any other.

And by drilling came mechanisation into farming, of which Jethro Tull was the father. He was the son of a Berkshire landowner, and was born at Basildon in 1674. He first invented a drill-plough, by which he contrived to sow wheat and turnips three rows at a time. He invented what was probably the first seed-drill at Crowmarsh, and perfected it at Howberry in 1701, getting his ideas from the groove, tongue and spring in the soundboard of an organ. By this means he first planted sainfoin (St. Foin), 'more faithfully than hands could do.' But his labourers were suspicious, disliked the engine and did their best to hinder his work. And it was not until after his death that English farmers adopted his methods, circa

1740. Of course, many blacksmiths have invented various kinds of seed drills, but with only local success. Figure 38 shows an eighteenth century hand-operated seed-drill, which must have been used much like the dibbling irons.

Then, in the order of work came harvesting, which until the invention of the harvester and binder in the early part of this century was all done by hand-labour. First came haysel, or haymaking, often done by gangs of itinerant Irishmen, or by the women folk who would all turn out for the occasion, wearing home-made poke bonnets with a valance for the neck. It has been said that very few men could keep pace with them. This was followed by the barley harvest, and later the wheat. Men worked in gangs, with one at the head known as the Lord, while his next in command was the Lady. And a custom which peristed for generations was the calling of largesse, to acknowledge a contribution by a stranger to the fund that provided the dinner at the Harvest Frolic. There were sundry customs regarding the last load from the harvest fields. In some cases they used to put green boughs and flowers, and sometimes a man would put a ribbon on the last load. And they would deck the last sheaf with a green bough and place it on top of the load. In other cases it would be the prettiest girl amongst the reapers that would deck the load.

The corn harvest was reaped by means of the sickle (a small toothed hook) and hook, the latter being specially made for the occasion, or a piece of wood so shaped, cut from the hedgerow and fashioned by nature. Otherwise it was done by the scythe, to which was attached a bail, the latter often made delicately and beautifully of wood, stopped and chamfered, with wooden teeth, as in Figure 34. In Worcestershire the scythe was a short handled implement of iron, with caither attached, not of wood as elsewhere.

The scythe, an implement of primitive appearance, has a vocabulary all its own, for it is either a riveted back or a crown, with its grass-nail, pole-ring, crewe, point and tang. While its handle, shaped by steaming, is known as the snead or snaithe, and the grips are the nibs. And there are many varieties, including the Devon which is 56 inches long, Norfolk, Irish Half Bright, Scotch and the Fenman's meak.

These were wielded with the utmost dexterity, made entirely by local smiths, with blades as sharp as razors. And the mens' waist muscles were in tune with their bodies, so they were able to work continuously from dawn to mid-afternoon without undue fatigue. The velvet lawns of England were famous long before the lawn-mower was invented, and these were cut by a special lawn scythe, the blade set at an angle to cut the grass close to the roots.

Beans required a special rake, and peas a special cutter, known as a Make. Tusser calls it a meake. A crop of peas was said to be made, and any crop, however severed from the soil, and left upon it to dry, was said to be made when in a fit state to be carried.

When the sheaves were carted five men were usually employed at the rick-making, viz., the rick or stack builder and the shutter-on. The three other men would take turns, one unloading on the wagon, another in the pitch-hole, and the third handing the sheaves to the shutter-on and the builder. The stacks would be finished off with those lovely corn-dollies, beautiful and characteristic examples of straw work following traditional patterns. Many of these would find a place at the Harvest Festival in elaborate crowns and regalia, in thankfulness for a good harvest.

And so after stooking and stacking came the cleaning of the surface of the fields, first by the gleaners or leasers, complete with poke in which to gather as much as they could immediately the gleaners' bell rung from the church steeple, until it rang again at the end of the day.

Then came the Dew Rake, alias Drag, Horse or Hobby Rake, which was used for a final clean up. The rakings after the sheaves or swaithes had been cleared were called dew-rakings, and were said to be picked up more easily when damp in the early morning. This reference to the dew is rather interesting, for the countryman used it quite a lot suggesting thereby early rising and a start before the sun got up. For example, in Yorkshire they spoke of the first meat in the morning as the dew bit; the piece of bread that used to be given to farm servants who went out early before breakfast was the dew piece; the heavy boots or shoes, oiled against damp, were the dew beaters, and was a name given to all early walkers. The first draught of tea or beer allowed in the morning to the harvesters was the dew cup; and stones such as limestones, that more easily collected dew on their outsides than other stones, were styled dew stones. In Suffolk 'dew drinkings' consisted of a pint of beer with a crust of bread and cheese that stood waiting for the men on the kitchen table at harvest time at five o'clock in the morning. Breakfast was at eight.

And then came thrashing, carried on most of the winter by the old barntaskers. In fact a rough and ready division of this thrashing was found in the personal pronouns—Me, Thee, Thou. One for own cattle, two for men's wages, three for the rent. For many a long year, indeed from when husbandry first began, this was hand-work executed by the Flail (Stick-and-a-half, drashel, nile in Gloucestershire, and Joseph and Mary in Breconshire):

> Thump after thump resounds the constant flail,
> That seems to swing uncertain, and yet falls
> Full on the destined ear.

Incidentally, there is more truth in this description than we realise today, for the steady drumming of these half-sticks on an oaken threshing floor had a music of its own, which has been likened to a marching host, or a cross between the hum of a mill-wheel and the beating of a big drum.

The flail has three sections, the hand-staff, which may be of hazel or ash; the swingel or tail-top, which is the shorter of the two members and was of thorn because of the knots in it; and the joint. The latter was most ingenious and varied considerably, being a universal joint with one or two parts. There was the handstaff-cap or cappel, otherwise the revolving wooden loop, which was fashioned of steamed hazel and was most difficult to make. There was also a middle band that ran through the swivel, and through a leather-bound eye on the swingel; this was usually of eel skin, or the underside of a horse's tail, bound together by horse or cowhide.

Flails were individual things, and to give the best results had to be suited to the hand of the user, not too heavy nor too light; the happy mean being about two pounds or a little over.

The middlestead, or midstey of the barn was usually used as the threshing floor, and the sheaves were placed end to end across the floor. Every sheaf was so placed by the fork so that its head met the corresponding one of the opposite line. Men usually worked in pairs, stripped to the waist, making alternate strokes, and it is said they developed special muscles in back and arms. They began work soon after four a.m., stopped for breakfast at seven or seven-thirty, had a mouthful of bread with a horn of cider (perhaps two), at eleven, dinner at one, and finished at four, thus completing twelve hours. Of quantities, a good man could thrash twelve bushels in a day, if the wheat was in good condition, and a hundred bushels of beans in a week. The heavier the crop the better for the flail. A poor thresher lost much of the grain, but with a good man there was not a grain left in the ear when he had finished. Incidentally, the floor must always be kept clean for the old hands, and the grain would be shovelled into the sacks by a wooden one-piece shovel.

Barley was the most troublesome, and for this a hummeler (*Fig.* 40) would be used. The grain was spread some three inches thick on the barn floor, and this contrivance was rolled over it in all directions. Another form was used rammer fashion, known as a thumper, huller, or chumper. These removed the ails, awns or havils of the barley.

Of the floors themselves, it might be said they were carefully laid, the best being of oak, and next to this, beech, elm was too dusty, but an earth floor was much more common. The best of these latter were laid dry rather than wet, as the wet were apt to crack. These were made of surface soil mixed with the strongest clay and dung, spread with a trowel and rolled.

Dry floors consisted of ordinary gravelley subsoil mixed with the chippings of free stone in equal quantities. This was sifted twice, first through a wide screen to catch the stones and gravel used to form the bottom of the

6

floor, and then through a closer one to separate the more earthy parts for the fine gravel. The finer material was then spread over the stones already laid, and the earthy residue scattered on the top of all. This would be about a foot thick, and when levelled it was beaten by a flat wooden mallet like a turf beater. Such a floor would last many years.

It was always the ambition to stack the bays or mows of the barn as thick and high as possible, and to this end a cart-horse was used to tread it down as it was unloaded from the wagons. In course of time the horse got high up, and it was no easy matter to ride it, although a boy usually did this. In Suffolk this was known as 'riding the goaf horse', and at the end the horse was let down the side of the heap by means of a double halter, with straw put down to save a fall. The horse slid down with some-one holding on to its tail to check it.

And then came winnowing, either by a hand-winnower, or by a fan which was of wood, turned by a handle, to revolve the flaps of stout sacking nailed to the axle of the machine. A sieve was erected in front of this, supported by an upright stick, which a man riddled as the corn was thrown into it by another man. As the corn fell through so the draught made by the fan blew the chaff outside the barn doors. These winnowings were known as flights, and barley chaff was held in great esteem.

And so the corn came to market. Up to the first World War the Corn Exchanges were held in the small market towns of England, but after that a tendency for centralisation set in and the markets moved to the larger cities. The local farmers would bring their samples of corn to the millers' representatives, who used the desks still to be found. And so the business was conducted amid that serenity that characterised the countryside. The goods

were delivered by the farm carts, horses decked up,
result of a pride shared by carter and farmer alike.

There are, of course, many other bygones associated
with the life of the soil; hedging and ditching which were
specialist occupations requiring, particularly in the latter
case, special tools. Ditching is represented in Figure 42
by the old one-piece mud scuppit (scuppit, an East
Anglian expression, is really a diminution of scoop). This
is made of willow or poplar, jointless, because being used
wet and left to dry, it would disintegrate if jointed. It
has a leather valance over the shoulder to keep the liquid
mud on the spoon, and the edge is reinforced by a fillet
of iron.

Stack-bases were in common use, usually made of
stone staddles, but in the village from which I write,
there are some of cast iron, evidence of a small local
iron foundry. The circular wrought-iron base was a
novelty, but has now gone for scrap. At the top
of the legs were bell-like foils to prevent vermin
climbing into the stack; and these when struck, rang
like a bell.

The shepherd is represented by the crooks (*Fig.* 41),
of which the finest came from Pyecombe in Sussex, and
to be extra good should be made from gun barrels. The
shepherd was the highest paid of all the farm workers,
bailiff included, and had numerous perquisites. Extra
pay for his help in the harvesting, and so much for each
lamb reared, and each sheep shorn. Even the lambs'
tails were his, and he was granted a cask of ale at lambing
time. Up to as recently as the beginning of this century,
his boy was known as the 'shepherd's page'. With the
crooks are a marking or buisting iron, and a clucket bell,
also a pair of shears, once used by a boy of fifteen to
shear a sheep at a county show, by which he won ten

shillings and the nice little certificate shown in Figure 33.
All these recall the lines by Barnes:

> Oh, I be shepherd o' the farm,
> Wi' tinklin' bells an' sheep-dog's bark.
> An' wi' my crook athirt my earm,
> Here I do rove below the lark.

The harvest-barrels (bever-barrel in Hertfordshire, bick
in East Anglia, firkin in S.W. England, bottles in Surrey,
and costrels), suggest some of the source of strength
needed in the harvest field, and without which the long
day's toil could not have been accomplished. They were
kept ready to hand in the cool shade of a ditch or hollow,
and are splendid specimens of the cooper's art. The
heads were usually of one piece of wood, and bore the
owner's initials (*Fig. 35*).

In the early examples the carrying cord or chain, was
of plaited horse hair. Gertrude Jekyll in *Old West Surrey*
has quite a lot to say about them, and remarks: 'a harvest
bottle when not too large or heavy, is a pleasant thing
to drink from, and when a fine labouring man drinks
standing, with his head thrown back, and his two arms
raised, the attitude is generally a strong and graceful
one.' If they were large a horn-mug was sometimes used
with them.

This brings to mind the labourers' food or wittle
bag, which was kept spotlessly clean, and filled and
prepared with a scrupulous ritualism each night by his
wife. It consisted of one large calico bag, known as the
wittle bag, into which went a bait bag, half the size of
the wittle bag, and a cheese bag half the size of the bait
bag, together with a meat cloth nine inches by nine
inches. These were packed into a frail basket, with a

bottle of home-brewed beer each side, held upright in the basket. The cloths were provided clean every Monday.

The faggot-cramp, (*Fig.* 36), was used in the construction of cattle sheds and shelters, made of whin bushes, wood faggots or heather. The faggots were compressed into shape by this simple appliance, and the shed constructed sectionally. With this is a stone-picker's hod, made by the village wheelwright, and often coloured as the wagons. The irksome task of picking stones off the fields was carried out by women and children. It was the firm conviction of many farmers that stones grew; however, it was a never-ending job to clear the fields of them. These hods were emptied into a waiting tumbrel, and taken to the roadside for the stonebreaker to deal with. He was equipped with a heavy hammer, wire goggles, a metal anvil often set up between the handles of his barrow, and a ring set in a handle with which he hooked the stones towards him.

NINE

THE MILLER AND THE MILL

YESTERDAY, and for so many centuries before that, the miller was an essential and extremely important member of the village community. So much so that he became proverbial, his thumb, his eye, and his prodigious strength which excelled even that of the blacksmith. One of his feats was sometimes to stand in a bushel measure and take up a sack of wheat on his back, for which he would have few rivals. Even his boy who learned the tricks of the trade entered into the tradition. 'I gave it him as it came from the mill', was a Suffolkism for straight talking. He was usually jolly, generally affluent and bore the prefix of 'Dusty'. All folks came to him, great and small, and from all he took toll, not exempting the gleanings or leasings of the fields. If you wanted up to half a sack of flour you went to the shop, but if more you went to the mill, and besides whole-meal flour (excellent for the preservation of the teeth), he provided pollards, sharps, fine bran meal; and in Gloucestershire gurgeons or rammels.

It was but fitting that such should be the case since his workshop was, next the church, the distinguishing and picturesque feature of the landscape; whether in the earlier mills by the waterside, or the later ships of the hills that twizzled in the wind (*Fig.* 45). It is sad that in these utilitarian days the element of beauty has departed, that where a mill survives it is too often but a memorial, and wind and water have given place to mechanisation.

A mill was of the elemental things and therefore close to life. Like a human being, a windmill might be left- or right-handed, usually the latter.

Surely the most important things in a mill, next the sails or the water-wheel, are the stones. These were in pairs, the lower or bed-stone, and the upper, or the runner, so named because this was the only one of the two that revolved. These stones are usually four feet in diameter, but there are some as small as three feet, and others four feet six, or even five feet. Since these are the part of the mill that do the actual grinding, they need constant care, and it is lack of men capable of dressing them that is putting them out of use. Their place is being taken by hammer-mills that will accomplish three to five thousand revolutions per minute, whereas the stones trundle along at a mere 140 (*Fig.* 43).

French Burr stones are generally accepted as being the best, but there are Peak stones that grind faster and wear out quicker, and Composite ones. The faces of the stones are full of interest and must be perfectly true. As wear takes place certain unevenesses appear which are denoted as *hills*, and when the stones are dressed these have to be levelled off. To this end a wooden bar known as a stone-staff is used. It is shaped much like a bannister rail, and the flat under surface is trued-up on a steel level kept in a long wooden box. If out of the true it is scraped with glass. The flat under-surface is coated with lamp-black or soot, and then passed over the surface of the stone, the black coming off on the hills and marking them out.

These stones are divided into definite areas. The central opening is known as the eye, and immediately adjacent to this are the eye-burrows; then comes the chest, which leads naturally to the skirt, or the outermost section contained roughly by the span of the hand. According to my informant, an old miller, the corn 'kibbles in' by the eye-burrows, the chest cracks it, and the skirt finishes it off. It should be further mentioned that the area comprising the eye-burrows is lower than the remainder, and according to old millers one should be able to lay a halfpenny on this, and the stone-staff should clear it.

These particular stones are further divided into ten quarters, triangular or fan-shaped, each consisting of a master furrow and two shorter ones. Between these furrows are the channels or cracks, known colloquially as *land*. And in dressing it is these channels that have to be cut afresh. The furrows have to be 'knocked down' also, otherwise they would 'grow up' and prevent the grinding process. And it is along these furrows that the ground meal or flour passes out. The faces of the stones vary in their cuts, those for flour being quite different from those described, which are for a grist mill.

The dressing is done with a mill-bill, or pick, an elongated diamond-shaped chisel of silver steel, set in a specially shaped handle, turned on a lathe. The hole for the steel is so cut that with each blow the metal is wedged by the assistance of a piece of leather. This is known as 'cracking'. Spectacles have to be used, and in the old days wire goggles, as used by the wayside stone-breakers, were the custom, fastened on the head by a piece of string; while an improvisation was often found in the two half-sections of a walnut shell, a small hole being cut in the middle. The time taken for the dressing varies from a day and a half to three days according to the composition of the stone. Formerly the stones were lifted by a hand-winch of ropes, and trundled off each other by thick wooden rollers. But nowadays a small crane is used.

Care has to be taken that the mill does not run empty
and the stones damaged by grinding against themselves.
The shaker or shoe that feeds the stones with grain is
kept in motion by an iron pivot known as a dolly or
wench. About this is a framework which supports a
bell known as the warbler, that is held up by the weight
of the corn in the hopper. As the corn is spent the bell
falls and is hit by the iron arm on the dolly, thus giving
the necessary warning. This enables other work outside
to be carried on while the grinding takes place, without
fear of forgetting the hopper.

Before the rolling mills came into use, the mill of the
illustration, which is a post mill, ground twenty stones
or sacks of flour a week and was very busy. The slackest
times being from June to after Harvest when the new
crops began to arrive. The slack season was spent in
cleaning up, mending and marking sacks, and doing
general repairs.

The round-house, which is merely a brick wall enclos-
ing the great brick piers on which the mill rests, is a
comparatively modern arrangement. Before that the
piers were exposed, and carts could draw in right under
the great central post, and be relieved of their loads by
hoists worked by the wind, lifting the sacks directly on
to the grinding floor.

Of the sails or vanes of the mill, it might be mentioned
in passing that these are of shutters or sheets. The more
common being the former, which can be closed when the
mill is required to work, and opened when it is out of
commission. The latter were furled when not in use,
and unfurled like the sails of a ship for driving. This was
known as 'Clothing the Mill'.

The position of these sails had a definite language of
their own, and could be used to give warning, or as

signals of distress. For instance, if they were set at a St. George's Cross +, it might be a signal given by the miller to the smuggler of danger in the vicinity, and after all they were all in that game; but if set at a St. Andrew's Cross ✗, it denoted all clear. The mill was also set at this when work was finished, and it is to be noted that most derelict mills stand with their sails so set. The St. George position was also a sign of mourning, or of trouble at the mill, and was thus used for a few minutes before starting to grind.

The miller's scales were not without interest, as indicated by the illustration (*Fig.* 46), that is of a pair that came out of a Suffolk mill. The beam is of the swan-neck type, dating from the late eighteenth century, or very early nineteenth century, and bears the stamp-plug of local Weights and Measures. It was customary for an accredited firm of scale-makers to supply the beam, while the swinging members were executed locally to suit the requirements of the trade concerned. The chair and the weight-plate are an interesting bit of local craftsmanship, the bottoms of which are from the solid. In the case of the chair the under-side has been scooped out into quarters and lead run in to achieve balance (*Fig.* 47). This has produced ridges forming a cross, which act as braces to prevent warping and splitting, which has taken place in the weight-plate.

The flour-boulter, once an adjunct of the farmhouse kitchen, was made to refine meal as received from the mill. The meal was emptied into the top, the lid closed, and a cranked handle revolved the brush set on an inclined plane over a fine sieve. The middlings came out at the side, while the flour fell into the drawer at the base. This came from an old Norfolk farmhouse that had remained undisturbed for over a century (*Fig.* 44).

On some of the eighteenth century Sporting Mugs, decorated as they are with a naïveté born of the soil, Toby sits drinking beside a mill, while hounds tear round the never-closing gap after the fox that shelters behind the handle. The mill is being blown into life by the visible breath of an angel. A delightful symbol, reminding us of our dependence on Heaven, once so apparent in the things of common life, but now passed into oblivion, taking with it so much of life's artistry.

TEN

THE COOPER

As other people have a sign,
I say—just stop and look at mine!
Here Wratten, cooper, lives and makes
Ox-bows, trug-baskets, and hay-rakes.
Sells shovels, both for flour and corn,
And shauls, and makes a good box-churn,
Ladles, dishes, spoons, and skimmers,
Trenchers, too, for use at dinners.
I make and mend both tub and cask,
And hoop 'em strong to make them last.
Here's butter prints, and butter scales,
And butter boards, and milking pails.
N'on this my friends may safely rest—
In serving them I'll do my best;
Then all that buy, I'll use them well,
Because I make my goods to sell.

RHYMING SIGN-BOARD, PAINTED IN
BLACK AND WHITE OVER A COOPER'S
SHOP AT HAILSHAM, SUSSEX, IN THE
MIDDLE YEARS OF THE NINETEENTH
CENTURY.

THE country cooper was mostly found in small market towns, though some villages possessed one often in the person or workshop of the wheelwright. He drove a lucrative and flourishing business which extended to many wares, catering for all branches of domestic life. For example, he made and sold churns, butter-washers, butter-trims, butter-tubs, milking-pails, cheese-vats, salting-tubs, dough-tubs, washing or dolly-tubs, and casks for storing butter, beer and cider, besides keelers for all and sundry purposes. He would also deal in turnery and general treen ware, including mazers and wassail bowls, clothes pegs, glove blocks, and articles of wood made to special requirements, including the great vats in the brewhouses attached to large estates.

Evidence of his activities and his stock-in-trade, are to be found in old records, for his products were treasured. The sieves or riddles of varying use and size; maltsters' and drainage shovels or skuppits, cut out of the solid; powdering-tubs in which meat was corned or salted; tilters and wedges to adjust the level of the cask as the contents lessened; and stoppers, which were wedges that kept the same casks from rolling; wooden taps, spigots or fawcets, ale-stools, chicken coops, and the various dainty little meal tubs of bent oak bands that stored the flour in the old farmhouse kitchens. He was indeed a handy man, and a fine craftsman, whose little harvest kegs, costrels, bever-barrels, or firkins are treasured possessions of most country museums. An allied or complementary industry was that of hoop-making (*Fig.* 77).

The cooper proper, or cask maker, worked partly in a shop and partly outside. He had a very wide range of tools, many curiously shaped, which included a short-handled, curved adze, and a side-axe. (The adze was man's earliest iron implement, used alike by the carpenter and the builder in shaping the timbers for the houses, and by the wheelwright for rough-hewing the hubs before they were turned on the primitive lathes.) It is true he had a bench, but he used that only to place his tools ready to hand, never to work at, carrying through the operations on the floor, like the hurdle maker. In the North of England, chiefly in mining districts there were Flying Coopers, who travelled about from place to place, carrying their tools on their backs.

A cask can be assembled and made in approximately 2¼ hours. Its length, girth and capacity must be exact, since it is made to contain an exact quantity, and it must fit together tightly and smoothly when the hoops are shrunk into place. Straight-grained 'mild' or slow-grown oak from the forest is preferred to hedgerow or gnarled timber.

First, the staves, which are riven by the broad axe, have to be dressed, which is done on a horse, similar to that used in some woodland crafts, on which the craftsman sits, the stave gripped by pressure of the feet on a pedal. The staves have to be alike, and fitted edge to edge, so that the joints are radial to the centre. For this the piece of wood is roughly shaped, cutting from the middle to the ends, giving it an inshot, or bevel on the edge, and each stave must be tapered equally above and below to the ends from the widest part. It is backed in the same way, and is finally hollowed with the hollowing knife.

The next process is jointing, when the stave is planed on its edge to smooth it in order that it may make a watertight joint when placed against its neighbours. The plane, or jointer, some 4 feet 6 inches long, is inverted and fixed face upwards, the stave being pushed over it by hand. As the edge of the stave has to be curved, the face of the jointer is curved to match, and is spoken of as a hollow jointer. Where straight surfaces are needed, as in the head, a straight jointer is used.

The next step is 'raising the cask', when a known quantity of dressed and jointed staves are taken and erected inside a hoop. As the circle is completed so the structure becomes self-supporting, and is placed over a fire of shavings and bits of wood burning in a cresset. After about twenty minutes of this heat, the wood is warmed through and becomes a little more pliable. A second iron hoop is now added, and a large wooden truss hoop which is not permanent to the cask, is driven down to the bottom, drawing it into shape. The cask is then turned over, and the runner or truss hoop (so called because it will run over the bulge of the cask), is knocked crooked. This gives the first narrowing of the second end.

A succession of wooden truss hoops, each smaller than the other, is driven on until the staves are all drawn together, and an iron hoop, known as the chine-hoop is put on to give the final tightening.

Now comes topping; the ends of the staves are trimmed with an adze to level them off, which is followed by chiving in order to make a level surface in which the grooves for the head can be cut. It is accomplished by planing round the inside with a chive, and this in turn is succeeded by crozing, which is done by another plane that cuts the groove.

The heads are made of oak boards, dowelled together by pegs, known in East Anglia as duels, trimmed on the straight jointer, and a circle of the size required scratched on them. Chalk marks are struck across these to indicate where dowels should be made. The side, or cant pieces, as they are termed, are cut roughly to shape with the axe.

The assembling process is of interest, realising the joint must be made watertight. A length of dried bulrush is split open and laid along the joint face, and the dowel pegs are driven through it, the next section being driven on to these pegs. Then comes 'backing the head', when the assembled head is chopped round to trim the square ends roughly to shape, and also to cut the long gentle bevel round the back.

The head is now laid in a scouring-board, which is a

flat board with an iron half-hoop across the middle. One end of this rests on the floor, and the other is held against the body of the cooper. He bends over it and planes the head across the grain with a heading-swift or topping plane.

Now comes 'cutting in'; the bevels on the head are trimmed finally to size and shape with the heading knife, the head being held between the body and the block, no vice being used for this or any other operation in cask making. Heading-up now follows when the heads are slipped into position. For this a spike is driven into one side of the head, the hoops are loosened and the head forced bodily into the cask. Then one side of the head is pulled up by the spike until it snaps into the groove or chine, all round, and the spike is pulled out.

The hoops so far used have been temporary ones of heavy iron kept for the purpose. The real hoops are made on a bick or beck-iron, which is an anvil mounted about 3 feet 6 inches high, and driven down to their final positions by a driver. The bung-hole is bored and enlarged to the size required by a reamer, a metal bush screwed in to strengthen the wood at this point, which is otherwise the weakest part of the cask. Incidentally, to remove the bung a flogger or mallet is used to spring them out.

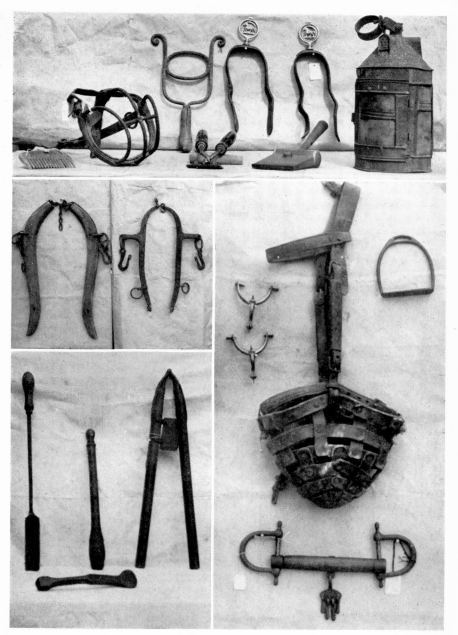

56. *at back:* Farrier's gag, swingle brasses, *in front:* Mane comb, night muzzle, clippers, singer, horn stable lantern.   **57.** Hames, to which the traces are attached (right of iron, left of wood).   **58.** Mouth rasp, balling gun, tail docker, horse medicine spoon (in front).
59. Spurs, horse muzzle, stirrup, check bit (below).

THE HORSE

60. Gig umbrella, gig lamps, dandy brush, hounce, curry comb, farrier's gag, sweat scraper, carter's whip. **61.** Cart harness bells. **62.** Horse's sunbonnet.

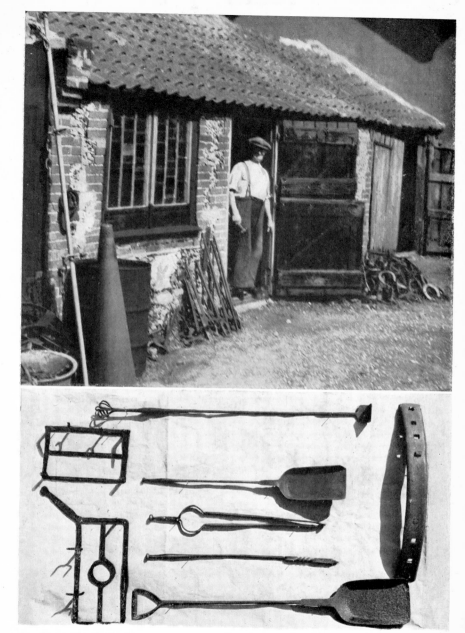

63. James Danford with nearly three and a half centuries of craftsmanship behind him, stands at the door of his ancient village smithy (sugar loaf mandril on left). **64.** Black-smith made: two trivets used on top of open fires, wrought-iron ash raker, hand made hearth implements, hand-made shovel, strake of wheel used as fender.

THE BLACKSMITH

65. The village shoemaker aged 80 seated on the traditional bench of his calling. The apron-piece of the bench is a drawer. (George Johnson Fenn of Bramfield, Suffolk).
66. Tools of the shoemaker: *left:* Lasting pincers, breast and other knives, fudge wheel, rasps. *centre:* Hobbing foot in socket and on stand, *right:* various awls and two rasps.

67. Carpenter's flail basket, panel guages, frame saw, pit saw (a pit saw is not a cross-cut). **68.** Boxing machine for making boxes in the naves or hubs of wheels. **69.** Wheeler's stool made of the natural bow of an apple tree. **70.** Wheelwright's type or bucker and spoke dog or cramp. **71.** Suffolk waggon still at work, showing butterfly chamfering, split baluster decoration and tooling to ends of summers and on bolster.

THE WHEELWRIGHT AND THE CARPENTER

72. Shropshire waggon (Tickenhill collection). **73.** Cotswold hoop raved waggon (Tickenhill collection).

74. The hurdle maker stands by a gate hurdle. 75. Woodman's horse for splitting broaches or spicks, using the wooden peg as a chopping block, bill hook, leather pad.

THE HURDLE MAKER

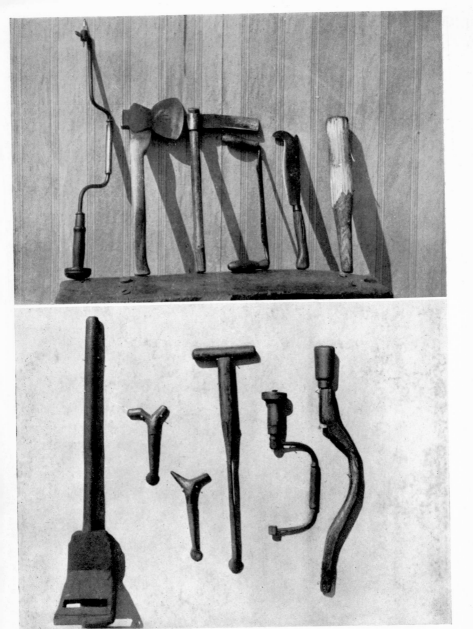

76. Brace, axe, thrower, draw knife, bill hook, mallet.　**77.** Hoop-makers' benders, two barking irons for the branches or 'wrongs' of trees, body iron for barking trees, iron brace and wooden brace made from naturally shaped piece of ash.

ELEVEN

SPINNING AND HAND-LOOM WEAVING

THE art of weaving is said to be of Celtic origin, and was known to Britons before the Roman invasion; in all probability it came next in order to flint-working amongst the earliest of man's industries. Certainly it brought great wealth in its train; first in woollen textiles and flax, which were endemic to our countryside, and then in cotton which was an alien plant that met a congenial atmosphere in Lancashire in the process of manufacture.

The stages of cloth-making are many and various, giving employment to large numbers all down the story. And, before the advent of the factory, and the consequent impersonal atmosphere, it is interesting to recall that it was a family concern with the weaving or wool-master living amongst his people. His capacious and lovely home (of which so many are to be found in Suffolk, notably at Lavenham), having his weaving sheds attached; and the taynter's yard where the cloth was stretched, hung from tenter-hooks (hence the name), being his own garden or courtyard.

In the Lists of Norwich Freemen, several interesting descriptive names for the various branches of weaving and its allied subsidies are given. For instance, there were Bedweavers, Dornyxweavers, Irlonder and Irlondweaver, Textor, Webster, and a Chaloner, or one that made chalons or shalloons, used for coverlets and blankets.

Then there was a Bleckester or Blexter, a bleacher; Calunderer or hot-presser; a Litster or Lyster, a dyer; Sherman, or a man who sheared the woollen cloth in manufacturing it. Slaymaker or Slaywright, a maker of slaies used in weaving; and a Tinctor or dyer.

It is interesting, too, to note how the industries impinge on one another, and become interdependent. The waste material of one becoming the raw material of the other. This is noticeable in weaving, because the process of currying and fellmongering calls forth much skill in removing hair from the hide, and wool from the fleece. This pulling and sorting of the wool demands an apprenticeship and an intimate knowledge of the material handled, for a sheep's fleece will yield as many as six to ten grades of wool, which in order are: First, second and third white; second and third grey; all used for woollen goods; then comes britch, which is used for carpets; and tailings which come in for stuffings, particularly saddles. The fleece of the sheep, which might weigh anything from 5 or 6 pounds to 13 or 14 pounds was rolled up in bundles of 28 pounds known as Tods, and the smell of the natural grease or yolk of the fleece was considerable.

The stages in order are—sorting the material into grades, washing and drying, willying, carding, spinning, weaving, fulling and finishing. All of which are well expressed in the following taken from the *Betts of Wortham* (the history of a family in a Suffolk village), circa 1806: 'George did not, like many of his neighbours, manufacture his own wool into cloth, but let his "whiting office", used for whitening yarn, for the sum of £15 a year. The various hand industries connected with wool then gave constant employment to the Wortham cottagers. In her schooldays Mary Betts had written out a list of wool trades carried on by the poor in their own homes—Staplers, dyers, pickers, scourers, scribbers, carders, combers, spinners, spoolers, warpers, queelers, weavers, fullers, tuckers, burlers, shearmen, pressers, clothiers and packers. One after another tumble, toss, twist, bake and boil the raw material until they have each extracted a livelihood from it.'

In further detail, willying is done by a small machine which disentangles the wool before it is carded. Carding sets the fibres all in one direction. Pandying or Fulling Mills were large square hammers that pummelled the cloth after weaving in order to thicken and felt-up woollen fabrics; and when dry these were teased over their surface by means of the heads of teasels. This is still done in the most up-to-date factories to fine merino blankets, as steel combs are too harsh.

Spinning, which has been described as an ideal cottage craft, gave rise to the old refrain:

> Two candles a burnin'
> And never a wheel a turnin',

and may be done either on a wheel, jenny or spindle; but it is the former method with which we are most familiar by reason of the picturesque and beautiful specimens which have survived (*Fig.* 53). It should be noted, however, that it was not confined to the cottage, for a wheel was in every home, high and low, and the art practised by rich and poor alike. It is a curious fact that our term of contempt for a thoughtless person as 'wool gathering' actually derives from the old habit of collecting wool from hedgerows and fences left by the passage of sheep.

The wool had to be carded, and often washed before

spinning, and the slivers (a mass of untwisted wool or other material) was lapped on the distaff. The amount that could be done in a day varied with the locality and the operator. It was usually a woman's job, and she might spin a pound in a day of nine hours, but the usual rate was an ounce an hour. The yarn so spun was always slightly uneven, and caused a slight irregularity in the texture of the material which lent charm to the fabric. On the other hand this unevenness could be overdone by an unskilled spinner which would result in lumpy places with thin weak patches appearing, thus reducing the wearing qualities of the cloth.

The yarn was then wound or reeled into a skein by means of a winder (*Fig. 55*), which is often confused with a spinning wheel, but which is worked by a little handle at the hub, whereas a spinning wheel is worked by a treadle, thus leaving free the hands to disentangle the flax to be spun. The winder worked in conjunction with a wrap wheel, or an adjustable wool winder, which was a stand to which were attached rices or runners. From the skein it was wound on to bobbins, which in turn were transferred to the shuttles. The cloth when woven was known as a web.

Dyeing might be done either in the yarn or the completed web, and these dyes were cultivated, such as the earliest woad (blue), saffron (yellow), or madder (red). Various local wild plants were used such as crottles-lichens that give brown or yellow colours, and grew on the stone walls of the Yorkshire moors; and weld—a specie of mignonette, also known as Dyer's Weld—that gave a yellow colour, and was found on chalky or sandy soils such as the Sussex Downs. Oak bark was used to produce a rusty, brownish black, and also for lighter brown shades; while Alder wood produced a reddish brown, and walnut husks gave a grey. Spindle-berries gave a beautiful blue.

Annatto was a dye yielding a fugitive bright orange colour, used in conjunction with other colours in the dyeing of silks, and in calico printing, and was distilled from the seeds of the *Rixa orellana*. Cudbear was a crimson dye, also made from lichen, especially *lecanora tartarea* with an alkali. Orchill, alias Archill, was another produced from *roccella tinctorin* and Rocella *fusi-formis*.

Dyer's greenwood (*Genista tinctoria*), gave a yellow dye much esteemed in the eighteenth century. It was also known as dyer's broom, green woad, wood or woad waxen. It gave a good green when mixed with woad, and Kendal Green owes its origin to the blending.

Another is Dyer's Weed (*reseda luteola*), also called yellow weed, weld, dyer's rocket, wild woad, or wild wood. This also gave a yellow dye and was often culti-vated with oats and barley like the clover of today, producing a crop in the second year. It was pulled and dried like flax.

The Looms (*Fig.* 52), often referred to as a 'pair of looms', in the old English sense, meaning completeness as in a 'pair of organs', were usually made of oak. Like all else of English carpentering it was individualistic, and called for a knowledge of weaving, otherwise the balance would be in the wrong place and the loom hard to work. Shuttles were even harder and more difficult to make, demanding fine and exact workmanship. They were often of boxwood with metal tips. The equipment of a weaver, besides the loom, were a warping mill, one or two reeds of varying sizes, threading hooks, shuttles and a bobbin winder, and a Raddle or spreader, for putting the warp on the loom. It should also be mentioned that the tenter-hooks are also used on the loom to keep the material taut, thereby giving a straight selvedge.

Hand-loom weaving was slow as compared with modern methods, as for example a woman could weave 50 hop-pockets a day, which was actually carried on until about 1916, while a man in the same time can now make five hundred. But there was great beauty and satisfaction in the art, weaving local material into local and intimate requirements which is exemplified in this quotation concerning a young woman of the mid-eighteenth century about to be married: '. . . with four feather beds made from feathers carefully dressed whilst she was in service. Twenty-two yards of fine home-spun linen, and twenty-two of coarse made for their sheets, and Abigail spun a web of diaper for towels, and one of Hugaback for tablecloths.'

Of the illustrations it might be said the Hand-Loom (*Fig.* 52) is reputed to have been made by a Mr. Garrat, a Lavenham joiner, for Roper's Horse-Hair weaving establishment in Water Street. The Hand-Wool-Combs (*Fig.* 54), were originally used in the cottages around the West Riding of Yorkshire. Across the room was a wooden rail, fixed about five feet from the floor, from which the fleeces of wool were hung. The comber sat on a stool, and holding the fleece in his left hand he combed down with his right, to lay all the wool fibres straight. Preparatory to this he heated the combs in a charcoal brazier which he had on his right-hand side to give ease in combing. These combs went out about 1820–30 but had been in use several centuries.

TWELVE

THE HORSE

Four white feet, you may give him away;
Three white feet, don't keep him a day;
Two white feet, you may recommend him to a friend;
One white foot, keep him to his end.

THE horse was for so many centuries the only means
of locomotion and draught, and the appliances,
trappings and gear pertaining to its health, comfort and
usefulness are legion. 'A horse! a horse! my kingdom
for a horse!' expressed more than the emergency need of
a king. Its decease was so recently as yesterday that it
seems strange to regard it as a museum piece, but such it
is. Almost all have gone, and what remains are but token
pieces — Shires, Clydesdales, Suffolks, Percherons,
Hunters, Polo and Riding Ponies, Cleveland Bays and
Coach Horses, even Pit Ponies. Shades of Tattersall's
and Aldridge's!

The horse's character, temper and idiosyncrasies are
the subject of innumerable treatises, while its value alive
or dead was considerable. The horse on the farm, the
ostler at the inn, the coachman complete with cockade
and fur tippet, the stage-coach driver, the village carrier,
and not least the horse dealer, have come down to us
bearing about them the aura of the stable. '. . . while
the other shampoo'd Mr. Winkle with a heavy clothes-
brush, making, during the operation, that hissing noise
which hostlers are wont to produce when engaged in
rubbing down a horse.'

The personality of the horse, its essential being, was transferred to those who tended it. The bow-legged, gaitered and breeched member of society, with a straw in his mouth, announced his calling with no uncertain gesture. 'Horse sense' expressed a certain rough and ready judgement that was right; while to be 'as strong as a horse' spoke of another trait in the human make-up. If the horse called forth cunning in certain of the lower orders (as for instance in that of the old dealers with a broken-winded animal for disposal, which he had carefully dosed with shot to stop the roaring during a deal), it also called out a wonderful understanding on the part of a kindly man. As in the case of the countryman renowned for his ability to deal with a difficult animal: 'Well, yew see, I strokes un, an' pats un; I talks tew un— an' I loves un.'

When Hissey made his *Tour in a Phaeton through East Anglia*, he saw over a doorway in Wickham Market, Suffolk, a sign bearing the inscription: 'Horse Gentler'. He was not slow to mark and appreciate that. It was the other end of the scale from the Horse Knacker, which incidentally, was also the name of the Collar Maker in Suffolk.

Being then so closely wrapped in the affairs of men, the horse has been the subject of a good deal of folk lore. It has been credited with the gift of second sight and an ability to see ghosts. It was an easy prey to the activity of witches who could stop a team at will and usually in the most awkward places, or cause them to plunge violently. This behaviour could be overcome if the carter carried a whip made from the rowan tree. And to prevent the horse having the nightmare, that is being ridden at night by one of these old hags, producing a heavy sweat, a stone with a hole in it was hung up near the manger. On the other hand, a number of the horse brasses, which made a fully dressed animal such a pleasant and proud sight, were undoubtedly in the nature of charms.

A horse's instinct has carried many a man to safety; and if it has betrayed some human weaknesses, as by those animals that stopped instinctively at certain pubs *en route*, it also often brought the driver home unaided after a hard day's bargaining at some distant market. He would climb into his sulky, fasten up the reins, fall off to sleep, and the horse would do the rest. Hissey, that great observer of the road, noticed the horses and their wagons coming home from Covent Garden in the early hours of the morning, and all the drivers asleep. Yet the horses would move to right or left of their own accord to prevent a collision.

Who, that was born in the years when horse-traffic ruled the road, cannot recall the musical clip-clop of the hooves as they rang over some quiet country road that was then white, the gig-lamps bobbing between the trees? And was not London manure one of the best products of the London streets, much sought after by market gardeners and such like? Not heedlessly was the horse described as the friend of man, which might recall the old Suffolk proverb: 'He who does not love a horse, does not love a woman.'

Amongst the things which have now become museum-pieces are the various decorations once the pride of the carter and the horseman generally. The sun-bonnet (*Fig.* 62) and ear-pieces to guard against sun and flies, and the rosettes made by the Horse Milliner. The hounces (*Fig.* 60) that were worn above the collar, set on the hames, trimmed with red or yellow worsted fringe and bedizened with brass. Teams carrying corn to market, or in any public display, were hounced. Hence the Essex word— *behounced*—'tricked up, made fine.' But the most beautiful of all, surely, was the Ring of Bells, set in a bell case of leather, studded with nails, and having a scalloped valance (*Fig.* 61). The cranked iron supports fitted into slots, or eyes, in the haimes or collar of the leading horse. There were four rings of bells in a set, and each one had four bells. But at Chichester the first horse had three bells, the second four and the third five. In the case of round bells they were known as rumblers. These were primarily used to give warning of approach when passing along a narrow road or lane, where two carts could not pass abreast, especially if there were no half-moon crossing places. With their passing has gone a lovely note of the countryside, although when first broken up they were often used as sheep bells.

The blacksmiths were closely allied to the horsemen, and many of these were farriers, but little removed from the vet. They not only shod the most valuable animals with the greatest skill, but could attend to inward troubles. The farrier's horse-gag was in their equipment (*Fig.* 56, 60). This was inserted between the animal's teeth, then turned upward to force open the mouth in order to administer a drench, or insert a probang, which was done through the circle set on a swivel. Other of their equipment was a Horse Mouth Rasp for filing the teeth when these grew sharp and prevented an animal from swallowing, and a Tooth Extractor, shaped exactly as those used by the dentist of those days on humans. Also it should be borne in mind that horses differ from cattle in that their food must be clean and free from dirt and dust. Hissey recommended that water should be given to them with the chill off.

The flexible brass band, with a handle at each end, was used for scraping off the sweat. Then comes the gig-umbrella with whalebone ribs, covered with blue drill; and a carter's whip with a cane centre, braided with thread, complete with thong, and mounts at thumb and end. The gig-lamps follow, one for candle and one for oil (*Fig.* 60). And not least, curry-comb, dandy-brush, mane-comb, and muzzle; with an implement for singeing in Figure 56.

There was also a night-muzzle (*Fig.* 59), known as an anti-crib-biting muzzle, to prevent restive horses from gnawing the manger woodwork, or the bars of a gate. And the check-bit used for colt breaking, the pendant keys resting on the tongue. Neither should one omit the horn lantern, used to light the way to the stable across the yard on a dark night. The wooden and iron hames can still be seen on farm horses, as also the old saddle trees, to say nothing of saddles, pack and pillion, spurs and stirrups.

We might conclude these bygones with the Sign of the Horse Doctor, still to be seen *in situ*, hanging from the eaves of a house in the lovely village of Kersey, Suffolk. It is either a stallion's or a mare's tail.

When the old drivers set out they always bore in mind the golden rule of the road, that was to carry in their pocket a piece of string, a knife and a shilling. Often too in that same pocket would be found a folding implement, that comprised a hammer, with a hook at the other end for removing stones from horses' hooves, and a small rasp at the side.

And here is an effort of the eighteenth-century epitaph writer, to be found at Haddiscoe, Norfolk:

WILLIAM SALTAR,
Yarmouth Stage Coachman.
Died October the 9. 1776,
Aged 59 years.

Here lies Will. Saltar, honest man,
Deny it any if you can;
True to his business and his trust,
Always punctual, always just.
His horses could they speak would tell
They lov'd their good old master well.
His uphill work is chiefly done,
His stage is ended—race is run;
One journey is remaining still,
To climb up Sion's Holy Hill.
And now his faults are all forgiv'n,
Elija-like drive up to heaven;
Take the reward of all his pain,
And leave to other hands his reins.

THIRTEEN

THE VILLAGE BLACKSMITH

My sledge and hammer are reclined,
My bellows too have lost their wind,
My fire extinct, my forge decayed,
And in the dust my vice is laid;
My coals are spent, my iron gone,
My nails are drove, my work is done.

SUCH is the epitaph to Jeremiah Easthaugh in the village churchyard of Darsham, Suffolk, who died on March 19th, 1788, aged 69.

Apart from its novelty as one of the better efforts of the eighteenth-century epitaph writer (possibly the schoolmaster), the words, though written at a time when no eclipse foreshadowed the blacksmith's craft, have become strangely prophetic. They serve not only Jeremiah Easthaugh and others, but all his successors and the trade which he followed. In the declension of village economy consequent on the introduction of the internal combustion engine, none is more apparent than in the case of the village blacksmith.

He was so essential that every village contained at least one, often two or three; and without him the houses could hardly have been built or the fields tilled. One might go even further and use the words of Holy Writ: 'For without him was not anything made that was made.' Is it to be wondered that the Greeks made of him a god? And it is not without interest to recall that a number of large engineering firms today owe their origin to a blacksmith ancestor. He not only kept the horses well shod and the farm equipment in trim, but made and supplied the utensils of iron for the housewife.

There is a blacksmith and there is a shoeing-smith or farrier and the two should not be confused. Yesterday they were quite distinct, but today they meet in one and the same person. The blacksmith is the worker in iron who made implements and iron-work generally, amongst whose notable sons was Thomas Tompion the greatest of the Clock-makers, while the shoeing-smith made the shoes and shod the horses, even doctoring them as necessity arose. He was far too busy to do anything else in the work of the forge; and in his kit would be found a probang for administering a pill to a horse, a rasp for filing down their teeth (*Fig.* 58), and a hook to extract them, identical to those used by the dentists before forceps became general. Hence his ability at pulling out the teeth of humans if they could stand the strain.

I was reminded of this by an old friend recounting his early days: 'I had a rare bad attack o' toothache, so I went along tew the blacksmith. He say tew me: "Come yew intew the traviss, bor, an' put yare backside on thet pail." When he had done, he say: "Yew dew look queer, bor! Gew yew orf tew the pub an' git yareself some rum, an' yew'll be orlright." An' sew I wur.'

And the distinction in the craft was symbolised in the leather apron, which they still wear, and about which hangs a good deal of interest. The apron of the shoeing-smith, which has a bib, should be slashed at each side, giving it what is termed tassels. That of the blacksmith, on the other hand, is slashed both sides and middle, and has no bib. And it all happened at a feast, presumably a Guild Festival.

A dispute arose as to the oldest trade which was claimed

by several, including the tailor, as he brandished his scissors. 'No, no,' shouted the blacksmith, 'before you could cut your cloth I made your scissors for you!' This was unanswerable, but it riled the tailor and he sought revenge. When conviviality had reached its height, he crawled under the table and slashed the leather apron which the blacksmith wore. And from then onwards the slashings have remained as marks of honour and distinction.

But there is another thing about this apron. It is recorded in old Suffolk sayings, that a woman once endeavouring to assert her innocence concerning something with which she was charged, made the curious statement: 'I should as soon think of wearing a leather apron!' This, it is thought, had reference to the Crucifixion; for it is alleged that the man who carried the Cross for the Saviour was a farrier, and had the nails stuck in his apron.

The patron saint of Blacksmiths is St. Clement, pope and martyr, A.D. 100, celebrated on November 23rd, the day following that of St. Cecilia. This, surely, is most happy, suggestive that the music of today is echoed into the work of tomorrow as beaten out on the blacksmith's anvil.

Amongst the customs in his honour and that of the craft, was one held at Woolwich. A senior apprentice was chosen to serve as *Old Clem* attired in a great coat, wig, with masked face, and long white beard. He was seated in a decorated chair, and wooden implements were placed before him, consisting of anvil, tongs, and hammers. A mate, also masked, with others, was in attendance. A procession was formed, old Clem being chaired, and they went from pub to pub chanting: 'I am the real St. Clement, the first founder of brass, iron and steel from the ore. I have been to Mount Etna, where the god Vulcan first built his forge, and forged the armour and thunderbolts for the god Jupiter. I have been through the deserts of Arabia; through Asia, Africa and America; through the city of Pongrove; through the town of Tipmingo; and all the northern parts of Scotland. I arrived in London on the 23rd November, and came down to his majesty's dockyard at Woolwich, to see how all the gentlemen Vulcans came on there. I found them all hard at work, and wish to leave them well on the twenty-fourth.' This ended in a feast, governed in splendour by the amount of money collected on the round.

Of course, not all the blacksmiths are dead, neither have all the forges decayed, but the outlook is not good. Too often the bellows are kept going by old men, neither does son follow father as in the generations now gone.

Not far from where Jeremiah Easthaugh lies I found his successor, though not in the old workshop which vanished long ago. Yet the present smithy (*Fig.* 63) was not built yesterday, and may even have been a rival concern to that ruled over by Jeremiah. He is James Danford, now nigh the age when Easthaugh 'lost his wind', who can trace back his blacksmith lineage in a direct line to 1603, when James I was king. Not a bad record that, and surely hard to beat in other crafts; but his sons have refused to follow him and he must therefore end the volume.

He was there busy at work making shoes against tomorrow, when Saturday would release some horses for his attention. He was without his leather apron, pressing on the rockstaff of his bellows in the old, old way, that ended in the traditional cow's horn, and using his slice in the customary deft and almost fussy way. I recalled the assertion that these old craftsmen can handle hot, almost glowing iron with impunity, owing to the callosity that forms on their hands. It was a tidy shop, too tidy, and he was alone.

He talked of his father, a stern and monarchial character to whom he was apprenticed: 'willy-nilly, and no schisms,' as he put it. Five long years, and two as improver. 'And if,' he added, 'they can teach this trade to young fellows in a few weeks, as they make out they can, then I was wasting my time.' His father's method was a look and a nod, followed by a cuff of the head: 'Dew yew want tew lame thet hoss, bor?' if he caught his son trying to force a shoe with defective clips on a hoof. He would look round his shop and soon note if anything was amiss. If, for instance, the water was low in the huge stone trough that ran along the front of the forge, he would bellow out to some poor wight: 'Yew want tew git up thare', pointing to the roof, 'an' take a tile off.' But they all knew him and his ways, and the trough was soon filled.

'Yes,' continued James, 'we made all kinds of things in them days—four-tined forks, shovels, gate-irons and window casements; and ullus at work. One o' our regular jobs was tew put new floats on the water-wheel at Wenhaston Mill. That was an undershot-wheel of iron, an' a nasty cold job that wur, the water a tricklin' all over yew. Then we had tew put an iron band round the round-house of the old post-mill there.'

'Did it have to go on hot?' I asked innocently.

'No, no, you couldn't do a job like that hot. We made it in sections and bolted them together.'

This recalled to my mind that every shop of this kind had its own special and local job to do. I remembered the old forge at Southwold (still there), where they made the irons for shoeing the old Beach Yawls that were a pride and peculiarity of that bit of coast. There was a little square port-hole in the walls each side of that shop and level with the anvil. The shoes were first made in two halves, then welded together, the ends sticking out of these openings. And it was there I spotted the moulds for the net-irons used in the local fishing boats. Another speciality of that shop.

I asked James Danford if he had shod any oxen, as I knew they were used at one time in the locality, but he said he had not. Then I mentioned how I had watched them shoeing horses in French villages, taking no chances and tying them up in cages. He said that was known as 'putting them in the stocks'. I remarked on the usual paraphernalia that is to be seen outside such old shops as his. His sugar-loaf mandril, for instance, and his iron wheel-shoeing platform. 'Ah,' he said laughing about the latter, 'two American soldiers came past here. One say tew the other: "What's that?" "Why thet's a gramaphone record, I guess!" answers the fust one.'

Inside his shop, to one side by a spare forge now deserted and crumbling, was an old brace (sway in Suffolk). This was held in position by a swivel beam above, to which was attached a rope or chain. When the bit was inserted in the usual manner, pressure could be brought to bear by pulling on the rope, and the brace was turned by hand. A crude but effective tool still in use in many of these old shops.

I came away as the sparks flew and the fire fell, and thought of the old motto: 'By Hammer and Hand; All Arts do Stand.' And the highest tribute to a piece of ironwork that we examine to-day is to say it is 'blacksmith made'. It is seen in the Hake or Fire Crane (*Fig.* 1), as also in an Ash-Raker that I possess, decorated by the spiral that was so much beloved by the old artificers. We have cause to wonder not only at their conception, but also their execution, for most of this fine work came out of wayside village shops, when art and life went hand in hand.

FOURTEEN

THE VILLAGE SHOEMAKER

THE Cobbler (chaucer, souter, sutor, in the List of Norwich Freemen), was one of the institutions in village life without whom the economy would not have been complete. He belonged to the honourable and ancient company of the Cordwainers, and his skill was derived from some five-years' apprenticeship in which he undertook: 'not to waste or lend his master's goods,' and in return was: 'taught' and 'found in sufficient meat, drink, board and lodging, washing, mending, shoes, aprons, and the use of tools.' Most probably his master would be also a tanner (in the old lists a *barker*). How old the calling can only be suggested by the fact he has found a niche in a Nursery Rhyme, which in turn suggests he was a busy man and bad on deliveries. He bore a close relationship to the Saddler and Harness Maker, also known as a *knacker*, but not to be confused with the horse slaughterer. The Collar-Maker, on the other hand, was distinct from either.

The Cobbler was enjoined to 'stick to his last' (which was also that which he threw at his wife), rather than run about after other things in which he was not skilled. But as the work was close and dusty he appears to have been prone to drinking, aided thereto by sundry festivals. For example, there was an ancient custom among them in Hampshire and Berkshire of 'Wetting the Block,' which took place on the First of March, some say on Easter Monday. This celebrated the passing of the Winter

Solstice and working by candlelight. The master gave a supper, which was supplemented by subscriptions drawn from amongst themselves and their customers. At the appropriate moment the block-candlestick was brought in, the shop candle lighted and the oldest hand extinguished it by pouring the contents of his glass over the candle.

Their whole week, however, was open to question, and has been described in colloquial Suffolk thus: 'Shummakers mak' St. Monday (i.e. take holiday); dew a little on Tuesda'; work hard on Wednesda' and Thursda'; begin to clean up on Frida' an' Sarrada'.'

Their saint was St. Crispin, on whose day Agincourt was waged:

> And gentlemen in England now abed,
> Shall think themselves accursed they were not
> here!
> And hold their manhoods cheap, while any
> speak
> That fought with us upon St. Crispin's day.

It was my good fortune recently to run across two of these village shoemakers, one in the West in Worcestershire (where the church has a crooked steeple), and the other in the East in Suffolk (whose church has a detached round-tower). Both were old men, my Suffolk friend born eighty years ago last December, and the other some ten years his junior. Their similarity was both fascinating and interesting. Alike they were genial, kind and philosophic, working as long as the day would allow, the Worcestershire friend by the light of his oil-lamp at which he also heated his irons. They were seated on identical benches, traditional to their craft, and both were using old tools, the Suffolk man those of his father, he of Worcester, those of an old forerunner—dead these many years—a noted practitioner in the making of Wellington boots that would slip on with the ease of a glove, but which needed a deal of wriggling to get off. And in both cases they were lone craftsmen with no successors.

Their shops were a study in contrasts. That of Worcester had a little pent-house bay with ancient wire-blinds that announced it was a 'Boot Repairing Establishment. All Kinds of Repairs Neatly Executed'; and, 'English Leather'. While the other was far less sophisticated, as one would expect in Suffolk, unchanged, unchanging, a true village shop, housed in a mediaeval compartment some twelve feet by five.

I first peered over the half-hatch door, and as I stepped inside, his old dog appeared to snuffle about my legs which I took to be an unfriendly welcome, but I was soon assured it was not so. 'She hev jist swallowed a wasp. She'll be all right in a minute.' And she was.

The floor was of brick, with just where he sat, two large blocks of wood set flush amid the bricks, all shining with nails (tingles and rivets), on which he rested his punyards as he worked at his craft. Curiously enough he was wearing a white apron instead of the leather one as used by his fathers (*Fig.* 65). At his feet was his lap-stone —a huge pebble from the fields—and by the door was his pail of water to soften the leather. Not in the true ancient style a brown earthenware pan, dark with tannin, but an enamel pail. His characteristic two-sided, flat-faced hammer, with an oval haft, fashioned for hardening the leather by beating. And his pieces of leather (rolled fleshes, cheeks, faces, rands, tails, and lifting and shanking pieces).

I asked him if he did any hand-sewn work, but he was glad to say that he didn't. He had done plenty, but that day was passed for him. He made the long waxed threads of flax drawn through beeswax and heel-ball, and fitted a bristle at one end to act as a needle. Made the channel along the edge of the sole, pierced the holes with his curved, sharp little awls (they called the Avocet the Cobbler's Awl in old Norfolk), pulled the threads through with great strength, and released his hands with a tearing sound as the thread left the leather mitten that he wore on his right hand. And when the sewing was complete the thin edge of leather turned upwards when the channel was made, was turned back on the stitches, covering them up against wear and tear, as one would turn in a furrow on a field.

On the other hand the Worcestershire craftsman had just made himself a pair of boots to replace a pair he had made in 1935. No other than his own work would satisfy him, and for that he would use bark tannages. His hobbing-foot was fixed to a huge block set in the floor, and was, as he remarked, a 'good tidy age'. His shop was cramped, hung round with shadows, but the gleaming soles of newly repaired boots lay like a harvest on his little counter. And I could not but notice in both cases how exact the work made them. The Suffolk man fitting a new heel to a quarter-tip with meticulous care; putting it on, taking it off, until it was just right and he was satisfied. The man of Worcester was for ever passing a rule over his work, as though it were a piece of precision engineering.

Unlike woodland crafts, that of the boot-maker demands a wide armoury of tools; various knives, extremely sharp, including a clicking-knife; last hook, welt pricker, pattern awls, welt and toe beaters of wood, nippers and pincers, including lasting pincers; hammers, awls, rasps, rand file, fudge wheel; and irons that need heating to spread the heel-ball along the sides of the heels, the edge of the soles, and on the instep (*Fig.* 66); to which must be added a slide-rule or size-stick, and a tape measure.

The old-time shoemakers were well acquainted with the idiosyncrasies of their customers, by reason not only of repairing their boots and noting how each wore them differently, but by measuring those feet for new boots, and transferring all the tender outgrowths on to a wooden last. And they were always concerned over their goods that they should be fairly treated. If you stood wet boots before the fire to dry and scorched them you would hear about it from the cobbler. An old country method to dry wet boots was to put corn or chaff in a dish, heat it in the oven, and empty it into your boot, thus absorbing the moisture. And I have just become possessed of a hot-water bottle of stone-ware, shaped to a lady's foot, that was filled and placed inside the boot before wearing, thus ensuring a warm foot (*Fig.* 28).

My Suffolk friend gave me his father's size-stick, probably a century old, and his father's slate, complete with pencils. On this was scratched the debts and rubbed off as paid. In the old days of village life you could get a first-class pair of boots, bespoke made, for fifteen shillings if you paid cash, and fifteen-and-six if they were put on the slate. And for those final settlements, which took place just after harvest, the shoemaker held a frolic and provided beer for those who came to pay. Some of the young wags would try to square off the extra sixpence by drinking as much as they could while they lingered. But it was not easy to do that for beer then was of the 'Tangle-leg' variety, as described in the chapter on

Brewing. Unless, of course, it was the 'Arms and Legs' portion of the brew.

In that Suffolk village of my friend, less than a century ago, as disclosed by the Parish Registers, they boasted a tailor, wheelwright, black and whitesmith, sawyer, cooper, thatcher, shepherd, ratcatcher, brewer and maltster, miller, cordwainer, collar and harness-makers, millwright, and amongst the farmers a husbandman. Not a bad lot for one small community.

One thing more; my friend's name is George Johnson Fenn. When I heard it I thought of an inscription on an old altar tomb in an adjacent village, where they are alleged to have laid up the smugglers' cargo under the very altar, and which also has a round-tower to its church. That inscription reads :

> Here is a stone to sitt upon
> Under which lies to rise
> To ye day of blisse and happinesse
> Honest John Fenn Clarke and
> Late Rector of this parish.
> Being turned out of the
> Liveing and sequestered for
> His loyalty to the late
> King Charles the first,
> Hee departed this life the
> 22 day of October Anno Dom.
> 1678

Families live long in Suffolk, neither would the inference of relationship be strained.

FIFTEEN

THE WHEELWRIGHT AND
THE CARPENTER

Here I am, both red and blew,
Ready for your work to do;
Use me well, and lend me not,
Cause if you do you'll suffer fo't.
Providence Protect Simon Pitchers.

PAINTED IN BIG LETTERS ON THE SIDE OF
AN OLD WAGON SMARTENED UP WITH
A COAT OF RED AND BLUE PAINT, BY A
SMALL FARMER OF METTINGHAM,
SUFFOLK.

JUST as the blacksmith supplied articles of iron for
the domestic and farming use, so the wheelwright
made and supplied those of wood; he also did a bit of
coopering. Certainly he made the coffins, as also the
travelling-box for youth and maiden when they left the
village home to try their fortunes in London; the maid to
service and the youth to some craft, perchance to the
Colonies.

In many villages the old wheelwrights' shops still
remain, and are as fascinating within as they are
picturesque without. They appear to have been undisturbed for at least a century, nothing thrown away,
nothing destroyed. Thick dust lies on these trophies
of past days that are thrust into crevices, or hang from
the rafters awaiting some possible resurrection to usefulness that has never come to pass. The windows are

festooned with cobwebs in a most delightsome fashion, taking on Nature's curves as they sag in serried rows. Here are the tools of yesterday; father's, grandfather's, even great-grandfather's. Moulds or templates, ancient appliances, gear of all kinds, await some final and inevitable doom.

And in most of these old shops, particularly those of Suffolk, there is a saw-pit, usually holding water; with perhaps, the old rollers still in position, slotted at the ends to take the lewers which levered the great logs into place. And, I am glad to say, they are sometimes used, the old saws hanging by in case. These saws, it might be mentioned, are not cross-cuts, as they only cut one way and that on the downward pull. In one of the pits I found an ancient tree that had arrived too late, for not now are these sawn up in this way, although the pits find a use for scantling long timbers such as required in ladder-making.

In one of these old wheelwright's shops that I visited recently, I found *in situ* a great wooden wheel that served to turn an ancient lathe. On this the naves were turned for the great wheels, though smaller work could be equally well accomplished. A boy turned the wheel by a cranked handle, and hot work it must have been. It finds an occasional job to do even now.

It is very rare that new wagons are built in these shops today, that ceased many years ago, but wonderful creations came out of them as each county testifies in its own peculiar and lovely types that still linger on a long life. A good deal of repair work is done, general village carpentry is carried out, even building. And it is good to say that the wheelwrights are always busy.

In the case of the shop of my visit a huge wheel was undergoing treatment. They had made that wheel sixty years ago in that same shop and had recognised it by a slight fault. Some of the spokes had been given to an apprentice to fashion, and before it was detected he had not left sufficient shoulders to the tenons or tangs as they are termed. (In the old days they were cut square, now they are round.) It was a technical rather than a serious fault, and they were duly thrust into the mortises, and were as firm as ever, but they served to identify work of long ago and by a hand then young.

Of the old sawyers, some of whom were travellers, it must be admitted they were a wonderful race of drinkers. Hardly to be wondered at if one was a bottom-sawyer. The top-sawyer was boss, and they would work for a day, perhaps two, then off to the pub, and oftener than not gone for a week. They would break down the great trees at which they did not earn so much money as at scantling (cutting up the sawn timber), as they were paid by the foot. This done, they would turn their attention to cutting out felloes, using the frame-saw for this (*Fig.* 67).

Pit-sawing of great trees was immense work. The cut had to be clean and vertical, and if it was not the saw told. Should the cut become hollow the blade would make a peculiar rumbling noise on its upward pull. At intervals to guard against this the top-sawyer would stop and drop a penny down the cut to see if all was well.

When the logs came in from the felling their ends would be daubed over with cow dung as a preservative. And it might be recalled that the old timber carriages used to haul them were known as Jills if with two wheels, and Drugs if with four. Then when sawn, the timber was laid up for a twelvemonth. This might be done by stacking the planks one-a-top another to the original shape of the tree in its own saw-dust, although this method often caused mildew. The more satisfactory way was to spline the timber, i.e. put little wedges between the planks, thus allowing the air to pass through.

A log destined to provide spokes would be riven into sections suitable for that purpose by the spoke-river, a tool common to many woodland crafts, also known as a froe, frow, froward, fromard, frammer, reamer, dillaxe, thrower, divider, side-knife and lathe-axe, according to the industry and the locality.

The wheeler's craft has its own glossary, for instance their outings were known as waygooses, and a wheel consists of a nave or hub, felloes and spokes. The floor of the wagon rests on longitudinal timbers known as summers, the ends of which are often nicely tooled; while the body rests on a bolster, also decorated.

The old wheelwrights (qwylwryghte), also did a bit of coopering, made various handles including stails or tails for rakes, hoes and pitchforks; snathes, or sneads for scythes; tillers for ploughs. And in turn would bore the elm trunks into tubes for the wooden pumps, that when placed in position had to have water-tight joints.

Most counties had their own distinctive colourings for their wagons. Those of Kent were usually cream, as also those of Berkshire and the Cotswolds. Yorkshire had a variety of shades, blue and white, brown and black, orange and lead-colour. Woodstock wagons were an ocherous brown, and those of Lincolnshire and Cambridge, black and orange. Dorset had blue-black, picked out with red. But by far the commonest colours are blue bodies, with red for the wheels and undercarriage that fades into a fleshy pink. Needless to say, therefore, in these old country shops are doors thick with generations of brush-cleanings, hanging like encrustations of some under-water flora. And you will be sure to find a paint-muller, not now used, that once served to grind up the colour on a flat stone.

Distinctive types of wagons called into being by local needs are the Radnorshire Gambo or Ground Cart, which is part carriage and part sledge; and the Morphadite of Norfolk and Suffolk that is still made. This is a composite wagon consisting of a tumbrel with shafts that pass through a forward extension, also with shafts, giving two loading platforms most useful in haysel and harvest. When not so required, the extension can be detached and the tumbrel used in the ordinary way. Another cart peculiar to Cumberland and Westmorland was the clog-wheeled car or tumbler, in use up to the middle of the last century. Early examples consisted of a few boards on solid wheels, without sides. The cylindrical axle was made fast to the wheels, which were $22\frac{1}{2}$ inches in diameter, the latter being of two or three solid pieces of ash, 3 inches to 4 inches thick, fastened together with cross blocks of wood dowelled on; and wheels and axle turned round together. The platform was kept in position, partly by its own weight, and partly by two wooden pins on either side of the axle; two-thirds of the cart's length being before the axle.

Ladder-making was another accomplishment carried out in these old yards. In the old days the pole for the sides cost 2s 6d and the staves a penny each, resulting in a charge to the purchaser of sixpence a stave. Thus an average ladder of 46 staves would cost 23s. Then the poles were cut down the centre by hand, but it was always a difficulty to get the chalk line marked out to the best advantage, and the pole was turned this way and that until a good line could be made. Now the poles are cut by steam saw and reach the yards in two halves, and those for the best results should measure 5 inches at the base, tapering off to $2\frac{1}{2}$ inches at the top. The line is then marked down each face and the holes cut for the staves by brace and bit, four staves to the yard.

Methods vary, but one maker will fix his staves alternately in each side, and when completed the two lots are joined into the ladder and knocked home, pegged with wooden wedges. This tends to lessen warping. The staves are fashioned with the draw knife, and the ends trimmed with the nug. Old craftsmen prefer oak staves as strengtheners, but iron ones are now compulsory, but these in their opinion let in the water, and it is there the ladder eventually breaks. The poles are of Scandinavian pine, since those countries produce the longest, quickest growing trees, ours being too slow, and therefore too thick. The staves are of oak from the butt ends of trees.

SIXTEEN

THE HURDLE MAKER

HURDLE-MAKING is amongst the old country crafts that still flourish in a quiet and undisturbed way, and whose products find a ready sale. Often tucked away in a peaceful yard beside the road it carries on in sheds that creeple and sag with the years, as though time were not. Changes may come in methods of agriculture, but there is little or no change in hurdle-making, although like so much else of countryside craftsmanship, it is too often pursued today only by old men. Needless to say it has its traditions, as also it has called forth its own particular tools and methods, and these, though simple, are as strong and enduring as its products.

A cobweb-hung shed with an earth floor provides the workshop and most of the work is done on that floor, no bench being necessary. A large block of wood acts as a convenient ledge on which rest the ash-poles that are riven by a tool with an upright handle known as a thrower, froward or helpmate and already mentioned as used by the wheelwright. The long block also serves the hurdle-maker to taper off the points of the uprights, or spiles, by means of a sharp bill-hook. Sunk in the earth floor, seven feet apart at ground level, are two wooden studs on which the craftsman stands his hurdle as he assembles it in order to true it up. The tools are hung up in the ledges of the shed walls, or lie about on the floor. These consist of a short-handled axe, hammer, very sharp bill-hook, draw-knife, and very wide sweep braces

78. Thatcher's needles, specially shaped leggett, reed hooks. **79.** The reed thatcher at work. **80.** Yokes (Jacks in Hereford, Knape or knave in East Anglia), measuring stick or spline, trimming board with trimming knife, bat or bittle, mallet above, leggett, iron pins, cutter, knee pads.

THE REED THATCHER

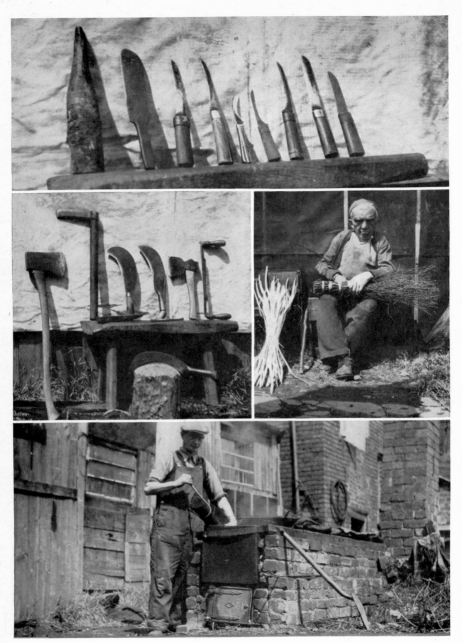

81. Mallets and various knives. **82.** Axe, thrower or lath axe, bills, chopping axe, draw knife. **83.** The besom maker lapping or wrapping a besom. **84.** Heating the poles in the Bosh.

85. Arthur Daines making the bottoms for agricultural skeps. The finished baskets are of peeled osiers on left and unpeeled on right. **86.** Tools of the basket maker. *back:* Bodkin, cane pinker, picking knife, beating iron, shears, beating iron, picking knife, shop knife, bodkin. *front:* Iron weight, bender for use with heavy rods, small bodkins, measuring rod across front, cramps at sides.

THE BASKET MAKER   155

87. Chair maker's tools: *top:* Five braces, one on left with spoon bit; *below:* Dividers and (**right**, reading top to bottom) Two travishers for finishing off the elm seats, the top one placed endwise to show the fine curve; a stock scraper or scarifier for cleaning surface of a chair frame; rebating knife. **88.** Shaving the billets on the horse.

THE CHAIR BODGER

89. The travelling tinker. 90. Velocipede with early wire wheels made by Joseph Tangye 1869 (Tickenhill Collection). 91. Packman's stick. 92. Penny-Farthing, also with wire wheels, dating from the 1870's. 93. Way wiser, pedometer or perambulator.

THE QUEEN'S HIGHWAY

94. Victorian baby carriage (Tickenhill collection). **95.** Wrought iron perambulator for peddling paraffin oil.

96. The potter with a half-built pot, two moulds set on a turn board. On the right is a jib mould on a pot board. **97.** Bow cutting wire, crucible, mouth mould, mouth ring, clay cutter, wooden scraper, pallette knife, jack knife or scraper, wooden beater. On the crude barrow is another clay cutter.

THE POTTER

98. The old hemp breaker. **99.** Roper's jack. **100.** Tops, used in making ropes by hand. The top 'lays' the three or more strands together. Oil pot, used in hand-hackling and dressing the raw fibre before machine-spinning of yarn became common. Winding reel for twine, used for reeling twine so that it may be more easily balled. Dressing combs, used for hand-hackling and dressing raw fibre, such as hemp.

made thus to eliminate stooping as much as possible. One is used to make the holes for the nails, the other to make the mortises in the heads for the ledges.

A picturesque contrivance set flat against the wall is a vice, known as 'the ladder'. It consists of a narrow channel formed by two pieces of wood placed side by side, slightly opening at the top. Into this head is inserted a tapering oak pole, hand-smooth with age, kept in position by blocks of wood that act as lugs. The poles are placed on top of this pump-handle-like appliance and gripped under a ledge at the top. Slight pressure exerted by the leg serves to hold this tight, and then the hurdle-maker shaves off any sharp edges by means of his draw-knife.

Gate-hurdles are of two kinds, those for sheep and those for pigs. They consist of four distinct parts, the *head* or end uprights, known as spiles in some parts; *ledges* or cross bars; *right-up* or central bar; and *braces* or slanting stretchers. In sheep hurdles there are six ledges, while for pigs there are seven, and the hurdle is generally heavier. Ash is the wood chiefly used, although sometimes elm, and 22 cut-nails fasten a sheep hurdle, while one for pigs requires 25. The nails are not driven into the head but against it, acting as pins. A good man can make eight hurdles a day, or four dozen a week; that is, getting his material from the pole-stack, cutting, fashioning and assembling. At the present time hurdles are £4 a dozen, but they have been as low as 10s a dozen when things were bad; their average price being 12s. Hurdles are 7 feet long, 4 feet high; the right-up is cut 3 feet 6 inches long, and the braces 4 feet 9 inches.

The hurdle-maker's yard is a picturesque entity of neatness and rusticity. The ash-poles lean against the upper branches of the shadowy elms, while shorter,

9

thicker boles are stacked in convenient heaps. Shavings mount up into a small stack ready for those who find them of great use for kindling. And there, in a gleaming pile, are the finished product, not now awaiting a purchaser, for they are sold before they are made, but awaiting transport to the sheep-folds or the farms. While about all is that fragrance and aroma which derives from newly sawn and peeled wood; the clean earthy smell of woodworking.

A generation ago there were hurdle-making contests at the County Shows. My informant told me the last one was at Ipswich in 1911, when nineteen hurdle-makers competed. The first prize was £2, the second 30s, and the third 10s. They were allowed two hours to make two sheep hurdles. One man made his in an hour, but he did not get a prize. He did not give himself time. It was my informant—James Tovell, now 78 and still at it—who gained the prize, taking an hour and a half.

We next talked of sheep. 'Ah,' said James, 'a good shepherd knew every lamb's mother. If yew cud reckun a lamb-and-a-half to a sheep thet wur a good fall. They used tew count thur sheep in an' out the folds like this: "Yew and yare partner; yare partner an' yew." I know they did,' added he with a grin, 'cause I ha' heered them.'

Besides hurdle-making, broaches for thatching are cut, stacked and split. For this latter operation a wooden horse is used, with a fat tapering wooden peg stuck up at one end. The workman sits astride, duly armed with a leather pad strapped on his right breast to take the wear of the sharp broaches off his shirt; strong evidence were it necessary, of the countryman's care and regard for the life of his clothes, and his general economical outlook on life. A sharp bill-hook is used, and the broach pushed against the blade. In the old days the thatcher made his own broaches, as he made his own hay-bonds. Stakes for fencing, and for garden plants, are also cut and prepared.

Prior to the 1914–1918 war, a large trade was done in hoops for barrels for the fishing industry; but this has long since ceased, other methods of packing the fish prevailing. For hoop-making a peculiar implement known as a *bowl* or bender was used. James Tovell gave me the one with which he started his career, and it has the distinction of having been cut, handle and base, from one piece of wood. The withy band was inserted in the slot of the implement from underneath, the foot pressed on the flat toe-piece and the handle worked forward, so that the band was bent into the desired shape. The hoops were made 7 feet, 6½ feet, 6 feet, 5½ feet, 5 feet or 4 feet in circumference, and fashioned in a mould or master hoop, two at a time, one inside the other and six for a set. They were sold by the 'long Tale', or six-score to the hundred, and tied off at their joints by means of an ash or withy shaving, no nails being used.

Various counties have varying names for these hoops, such as Swinger, Middlin, Long and Short Pipe, Killiken, Firkin, Long Pink and Short Pink in Hampshire; and in Sussex and Kent: Footers, Middlings, Long and Short Pipe, Ten Foot, Hogshead, Nine Foot, Barrel, Eight Foot, Kilderkin, Seven Foot, Firkin, Six Foot, Long Pink, Five Foot, Short Pink and Tumbril; the sizes reading downwards are from 14 feet to about 4 feet.

SEVENTEEN

THE REED THATCHER

Thatcher, thatcher, thatch a span,
Come off your ladder and hang your man.

ON a Suffolk by-road I came across a thatcher by the name of Edward Sallows repairing the thatch on a picturesque pair of cottages with old reeds taken from a barn that had been blown down. A man with such a name, and one known to have derived from a long line of thatchers (thaxters, thackisters, reeders), and gardeners, might well claim to be a descendant of one who practised the craft when surnames were first distributed. He is now 74, and has pursued that calling all his life, following his one-armed father who, in spite of such a disability, was a master of his craft; but he has no son to follow him.

Like so many other country crafts, thatching has only a simple armoury of tools, and Nature provides the materials. But great art goes into the work in which tools and materials meet and make a covering of enduring beauty for man's head against the tempest and the heat.

Being an East Anglian, with all the inheritance of ronds and wind-swept reeds, Edward Sallows naturally talks in terms of reed rather than straw. Reed lasts longer, gives a better job, and in every way is more satisfying. Straw has to be used for the ridges as it lends itself to ornamental work, and if straw, then that from rye rather than from wheat or barley, it being tougher, working better and creating a good finish. It has to be pulled or gavelled, yelmed, helmed or gabbled according to the locality, before it can be used.

The reeds are tied up in bolts, five bolts making a fathom, which should measure six feet in circumference. They look picturesquely mellow and mealy, lying in rows, with their hollow tubes packed tightly like a huge honeycomb. The thatcher dresses them on his dressing-board, and trims them with his cutter used saw-fashion, cutting off their feathery tops when necessary.

Starting, equipped with his knee-pads, at the eaves, he works upwards until the ridge is reached. If he is repairing an old thatch, all the perished reeds are removed and new ones carried up the ladder by means of yokes (jacks in Hereford), and laid in position. These yokes are of hazel, hinged at the base by string, notched at the top and fastened with a corresponding loop of string; they vary in style according to the district and are known as jacks, knaves, stroods or frails. In the case of a house, if the old reeds are held in position by tar-spun yarn, the thatcher knows they have been there since it was built, or at least since before ceilings were added, which may be anything up to two hundred years. The new reeds are laid a bolt at a time, side by side, and fastened securely by long, whole hazel or willow rods known as sways or liggers. These are placed across the reeds and held down by iron reed hooks, which are hand-made, of varying lengths, and driven but lightly into the rafters, which are located by long iron rods known as pins.

The most characteristic tool of the thatcher is the legget (a word probably derived from *Legge*—to lay), also known as a drift in some districts. This is in constant use for patting the reeds into position and making them nice and even, and is also employed in working the reeds into such designs as they will allow. For this latter purpose the round-headed example in the illustration has been specially fashioned. The heads of these implements are of poplar, because it is more fibrous than other woods, and does not split, and are studded with horse-shoe nails driven home to within half-an-inch of their heads. The handle is of ash. Another tool, roughly fashioned out of a piece of hard wood, is the sputtle, a flat bat-shaped instrument that serves to tuck the reeds under those above them. It is known as a crammer in Gloucestershire, and a bittle in the West Country. Nor must I omit to mention the needle, a sizeable object that would serve equally well as a poker (*Figs.* 78, 80).

When the ridge is reached it is finished off by a characteristic process known as roving, for which special split rods with blunt ends called rovers are used. These are laid along the ridge and fastened down by means of broaches (sprays, specks, spicks, in the Cotswolds, buckles in Worcestershire, spurs in Wessex). These broaches, the ends of which are spiked, not only serve to fasten the thatch to the roof securely, but also add charm and character to the finished work, being arranged into a pattern known as diamenting. Trimming knives, often fashioned from an old scythe-blade, serve to trim the eaves true and neat, and also cut the interesting and characteristic scallops that adorn the ridge. This work it should be noted is done by hand and eye working in unison, no templates being used.

For an average-sized farmhouse it may take anything up to two thousand bolts of reed, which a short time ago cost a shilling each, but now cost three shillings. Sways are made up and sold in bundles of sixty for six shillings, whereas they were one-and-sixpence. Rovers are tied up in bundles of one hundred, and now fetch seven-and-sixpence, and broaches, tied up in bundles of two hundred are sold by the thousand at twenty-five shillings a thousand. These increased prices have naturally sent up the cost of the finished work, which is estimated by the square, that is a hundred square feet. This is measured by the thatcher's spline, a flat measure marked off at every six inches. In the old days a man worked as long as he could see, from six o'clock in the morning until nine at night, and he would complete the thatching of a farm house roof in three or four weeks.

Needless to say, a family engaged in this pursuit for so many generations has its accomplishments to recall, and its outstanding feats to acclaim, achieved by some member who left his mark. In Edward's case it was by his grandfather, a wonderful craftsman in his day whose work was much sought after. He was once consulted by a farmer who greatly loved a thatched house, but as greatly feared fire. 'Now,' said grandfather, 'I'll undertake to thatch your house for you, and when I've done I'll take a pailful of hot coals and pour them down the thatch from the ridge, and I'll guarantee that it will not burn.' This was carried out as agreed, nor was there a fire. On another occasion he laid a barn with new reed, and when he had finished, in the thatch, plain for all to see was a wagon and horses: 'That was a pretty sight, if you like!'

EIGHTEEN

THE BESOM MAKER

Here's a large one for the lady,
And a small one for the baby;
Come, buy, my pretty lady,
Come, buy o' me a broom.

BESOM-MAKING is a woodland craft, and it is but natural that we should look for such an industry on the edge of a great forest, or what was once a forest. I found mine therefore, at Bewdley, Worcestershire, within hail of the Wyre Forest.

It is but fitting also, that this yard of the besom-maker should be in old Bewdley, rather than the new. Down by the water-front of the Severn lies the new eighteenth century Bewdley, dominated by its church; but here, on the steep slopes of Wyre Hill, smacking of mediaeval England, amid ancient inns, such as the *Black Boy*, is the old Bewdley, one of the English gateways into Wales and seat of the ancient Council of the Marches. Up and down this water-scored trackway went the pack-horses carrying the raw materials for the Bewdley industries: bark for the tanning, charcoal for the furnaces that smelted pewter and brass, horn for the button-makers and the horn workers, flax for the rope-makers, clay for the potters, leather for the cordwainers and cloth for the cappers.

Decay characterises much of Wyre Hill, and has eaten deeply into the old red bricks of its homesteads that lie tumbled on its tracks. Yet the cottage homes, littered with so many memories, speak of a prosperous and contented life. Children gambol on the slopes—the youngest ones contained within their home-made barriers set across the doorways—and the family dogs come out and sniff at passing strangers as they have done through a long and untroubled history. Wyre Hill to-day is much as it was of old.

And so in the old besom-maker's yard, changed not one whit since old Mrs. Bishop, mother of Albert Bishop, died, and the business was turned over to her son-in-law, Christopher Birch, who now also has passed on at a good old age. Here are the old wooden sheds, with earth floors, here the old bosh in whose length the oak poles are boiled and steam through their covering of old sacks. And here in the middle, towering upwards, capped by its corrugated-iron roof, is the Dutch-barn-like affair in which the birch twigs are stored. Were the roof but of thatch, one could record no change since Elizabeth was Queen, or since Prince Arthur was betrothed to Catherine of Aragon at Tickenhill within bow-shot eastwards.

Like the implements of other woodlanders, the tools and equipment of the besom-maker are simple and few (*Figs*. 81, 82). The chief qualifications for the successful pursuit of the calling are patience and supple fingers. Given these, some characteristic bill-hooks with the funniest little kick of a handle, like the spurs of a fighting-cock (I believe they are technically known as fawnfeet, and assuredly they are taken out of the hedgerow), knives that are bitten into crescents through patient wear, and are as sharp as a surgeon's scalpel; a lathe-axe that has other names in kindred callings, such as that of the wheelwright and the hurdle-maker; a home-made peg-like mallet; and a vice or break fashioned out of the natural fork of a tree; and you have all that is needed.

The birch twigs are cut from October to May, and are

made into two distinct types of besoms; one for brooms and the other for the making of vinegar. Besides birch, heather is largely used in localities where it is more common, and ling, which makes a softer broom than heather, and was much favoured by the miller for use in his mill.

The brooms are bound with strong, pliable lithe shavings from the oak poles, known as laps or bonds, made workable by heating in the bosh (*Fig.* 84), and tied like a tape. These are sometimes made from willow, and it is in the tying that the skill lies, for the fastening must last as long as the broom. Split-cane has been substituted, and also wire, but the latter is never used by the best besomers. Hazel poles form the handle, shaved by the draw-knife and held in the break. These brooms are in request for many purposes, not forgetting garden work, and also in the iron works for sweeping away the slag that forms on the surface of the hot metal.

Although besom-making seems a simple and easy business, like so much else that is apparently simple, for example hurdle-making, it takes a long time to learn, and appears to run in families with long attachment to the soil.

The vinegar besoms are cut both ends square, two feet long, and for this a measuring stick is used made of a hazel rod, half of which is peeled and half left unpeeled, forming a picturesque and characteristic gauge. They are placed in the vats, butts to twigs, to a depth of three feet, and serve to aerate, filter and create acetic acid in the malt liquor; they are also credited with giving the vinegar a subtle flavour. When the vats are cleaned the sludge that remains in the besoms is thick beyond imagining. Another use for these birch bundles, for such in reality they are, was in the manufacture of steel-plate. They were strewn lightly on the red-hot surface when the plate came in contact with the air and their consumption reduced the oxidation that then took place.

Besides besoms, wiskets (swills, spelks, slops or skips elsewhere, to which might be added Sussex trugs), are made in this Wyre Hill yard. These are of three sizes, with rims of hazel, called bools or bows, to which plaited oak lathes, or chises, are attached in exactly the same way as in the coracles that once plied on the nearby Severn. Here they are largely used as coal buckets, and beautiful craftsmanlike containers they are. The laths, thin and pliable, are taken from the oak poles after these have been boiled in the bosh. They are prized off with gentle pressure of a sharp knife along the grain of the wood, which has been made supple by soaking in the hot water. (When the bosh is in action it gives off a healthy, aromatic and slightly astringent odour of tannin, good to inhale). Clear water is used and brought to the boil, and the poles are left in soak for twenty-four hours or longer. The bark comes off whole, like the covering it is, and will stand on end, making a hollow tube. This, with the chippings is used for firing.

There is something about this yard in old Bewdley that seems eternal. Yet another generation plays about the birch stacks, in and out of the sheds, taking it all for granted. A hog-stool rests under the shade of the wood shed, suggestive of numberless forerunners of the pig that grunts and rootles about the orchard; geese raise the alarm and see the stranger off the premises. And Albert Bishop, kindly and genial, as is characteristic of besom-makers, his calling behind him, sits and surveys the littered yard of his fathers and all his years.

NINETEEN

THE BASKET-MAKER

I can rand
At your command,
*　　Put on a decent border;*
Upsett tight,
Wale all right,
*　　And keep my stakes in order.*

THE art of basket-making is very widespread, and suffers less eclipse than some of the other woodland crafts, because it is peculiarly adaptable to the blind, and cannot be done by machinery. However, there are signs of declension, not by reason of mechanical methods of production, but by the creation of substitutes for wicker, notably paper pulp on a wire core. Yet something of a mechanical peeler, or engine, has appeared on the scene, once the prerogative of women. So far this has been chiefly used by the large makers, the small man preferring the old hand method of the break set on a post or stump.

It is good to think that we have this age-old industry still with us, for its origins are lost in time, and vie with the flintwork of Neolithic ages for advantage in seniority. In far-off days man made his housen of wickerwork, was buried in a wicker container, as he had been cradled in such, and reared his temple of that same fabric. Tennyson refers to this in writing of the building raised by Joseph of Arimathea at Glastonbury:

And there he built with wattles from the marsh
A little lonely church in days of yore.

And similarly, when man ventured on the great wide waters, it was in a coracle which was but another basket slewed over with skins. As he pushed off from the shore, it was into a world whose narrow bounds were fast set in mystery and amazement.

It was but fitting therefore that I should meet one of these basket-makers (skepperers), in an ancient village in that old world of Suffolk, where Time is not and where the years do not change. It was but a few miles from the great North Sea. Here, in a tiny hamlet, with a church as magnificent as a cathedral, standing in what was once a clearing in a great forest, on the site of a pagan shrine, this man plies a trade that was known and followed when human sacrifices were probably offered on an earlier altar.

Even the present church, old enough in all conscience, was not built yesterday. Dean Colet was once its rector, and must have looked on its furnishings (now as then in all their rarity), as a heritage to be cherished. Neither were the alabaster effigies of Knight and Lady on their alabaster tomb any newer than they appear today. For the knight was in the field with Henry at Agincourt on St. Crispin's day. And as I watched the craftsman deftly weaving the bottoms for agricultural skeps (using the old word), time played a trick. I thought he was on war-work, making shields for the King's bow-men, to the order of that same knight. Time, place and calling were equally ageless.

Like so many of these country crafts basket-making was a family business. Son followed father all down the long years until all the members of the family were involved. The only outstanding relations were those who left it to follow something easier, such as soldiering or becoming the parish constable.

The armoury of tools is small (Fig. 86), consisting of a

characteristic beating iron, bodkin, shears, shop-knife (fashioned from a table-knife), and a picking-knife. This latter, with the beating iron, appears on the Arms of the Basketmaker's Company, and has altered but little down the years. Then come blocks or cramps for square work, a measure knotched off in inches with a cross set at each six, which for use by the blind is marked with little brass studs, a larger one at each six inches. There are hoops of wood varying in size, like a girl's hoop, to set over the stakes to keep them in order during the up-setting. Add to these a board on which to set the embryo basket, and a weight, often the base of a flat-iron, to set inside the basket in its earlier stages to give it a balance as the work proceeds, and you have the lot. But to these must be applied the skill and deftness of fingering, which perhaps explains something of the aptitude of the blind for this work.

I asked if the work was hard on the hands, to be told that his daughter had never found it so. She would come home from school, sit on the bench, and make 'as pretty a little basket as you could wish to see'. But when his son left the craft to serve his country, he found it very different on his return. His hands suffered very much until use and custom gave them again the necessary hardness and callosity.

Osiers, the raw material of the basket-maker, are of many kinds. They are known as rods in Norfolk, osiers in Suffolk, and withies in Somerset. They are cut every year from October onwards through the winter months, by a dexterous use of a bill-hook, with a sharp upward movement. Those to be peeled are stood in six inches of water, until they begin to sprout roots and the sap rises, which is in the spring of the year. They are peeled during April and May by being pulled through a break, enough for a twelve-month's supply. The various kinds of osiers form themselves into three groups, viz. buff, which are boiled in a tank; peeled and un-peeled. Water in which willow withes have been soaked has great staining qualities. The Suffolk author of *Margaret Catchpole* tells of a boy—Charles Stegall—leaving home and joining a gypsy encampment nearby. Search was made for him amongst the tents but he was not recognised as he had been washing in this water, becoming brown in consequence. However, when found he was put to school and afterwards became a very much respected clergyman of the Church of England in a nearby parish.

Local varieties best known are Dickey Meadows (from one Richard Meadows of Mawdesly, Lancs.), Black Maul, Black Spaniard and Black Sally in Worcestershire; Clay and Stone Rods in Gloucester, Worcester, Hereford and Warwick; Black and White Newkinds in Yorkshire and the Fen Country; Brown Hollands, Glibskins and Red Rods in Cambridgeshire; Bent and Yellow Willows at Rye. Then there are Longskins, Silverskin, Black Top, Merrin; Black, White, Green and Yellow Osiers, in a list too long to include all. In Suffolk sallow was a term used for any soft-wood, such as birch, alder, hazel or willow of any variety. They are cultivated in bolts or garths.

The first stage in basket-making is 'tying the knot', which is in the centre of the bottom of the basket to be made. I took up the wheel-like bottom of the skep he was fashioning and noticed that four stakes were laid on three at right angles, and were being tied and interlaced together with one peeled stake which when bent into position gave another spoke to the wheel, making fifteen to the circle. When the bottom is finished the next stage is up-setting. Stoutish stakes are taken up one at a time, the ends pointed with the knife, a hole or opening is made in the edge of the basket bottom with the bodkin, the shaved ends of the stake driven in and then bent upwards at a right-angle. These stakes are set about two inches apart. Then the walls are either randed, slewed or waled, according to the quality of the work.

Randing is done with single osiers and is the most expensive method. Slewing is done with two or three osiers together at a time; while waling is to work inside one, outside two, or two and two. Then comes the border as per the rhyme, otherwise the rim; handles or openings for the hands, as in the case of pigeon baskets; and trimming, which is done with the sharp picking-knife. And that is all.

My informant specialised in all kinds of agricultural baskets, including malting and dung skeps, the latter for use at Newmarket. He also made wattle hurdles to almost any size, suitable for garden fencing, a durable and artistic enclosure, forming an excellent background. These are made from stakes too large for baskets, on a bowed log called a mould, in which are mortises to take the upright poles. Chair-caning is also done, and the cane for this work is split by a small engine that much resembles a plane, the iron being set at such an angle as to accomplish the splitting to the size required.

His yard was as full of interest as it was full of tanks and shallow basins in which the bolts could be placed to absorb the moisture and keep them supple for working. This is known as pitting. The various kinds of willows in bolts (about two hundred to the ton), were housed in sheds that gave out a lovely, mealy smell as one entered, stepping over the leafy peelings. Once upon a time, in that fine rural economy, these peelings were not wasted, but were transferred to the pigsties for bedding. Now they lie in lovely russet heaps prior to being burned. A few years back he had as many as twenty women working for him in the season, peeling the rods, but now they are too well off to need the extra money and this casual employment.

It is good to think that here, in this secluded and historic village, this rural craft flourishes exceedingly and that the next generation keeps pace, and they have more than they can do.

TWENTY

THE CHAIR-BODGER OF THE CHILTERNS

TO live in a Birket Foster cottage of old faded red brick, thatch and timber, grass running up to the walls, surrounded with flowers and fruit trees, must count for something. If the quarters are cramped, the windows small, they speak of a deep peace, contentment, and roots that run long and far into the English soil and the English character. Here is life arcadian, that for which the soul yearns, and where the years linger. Sentiment may have its say, but here is reality. Added to this, to find one's livelihood in adjoining woods, to be one's own master, to work as long as the day allows. and to be lonely, is bliss indeed.

I found the bodger's cottage on the edge of a green, surrounded by woodlands, before I found the bodger. His old black mare, housed in a lean-to at the side, was glad to see me, and nuzzled up in a friendly way to greet a human. She too, represented the old way of life, when the woodman hawked his wares in the nearby township in an endeavour to sell his legs to the chair-makers; as these in turn hawked the finished chairs to shops in London and nearby market-towns.

Of all the woodland crafts, that of chair-bodging seems the most rural. Away from village and town alike it is carried on in perfect rusticity, set in the peace of the lovely beechwood glades. The passing stranger has to seek it, and he might be within a few hundred yards and yet miss it, and all that it represents. However, one guide may be his—the trail of saw-dust often laid to lead the bodger homewards out of the woods on a dark night. The origin of the name seems to be obscure, but it may be a variant of *Badger*, a now obsolete term for a pedlar or huckster, particularly one who bought up farm-house remainders of produce such as butter, cheese and eggs, and then hawked them for sale.

It is good to think the old craft still pursues its way, but for how long one hesitates to say. There is plenty of market for the finished article; and as my informant told me with a grin, never before in his history had he been told his prices were not high enough. But that had happened to him under the regime of controls. And the survival is not so strange as it may seem on other grounds, for a skilled man can produce today, by these primitive methods, as many chair-legs, if not more, than a machine, which is saying a lot. Once again it is a family inheritance, father handing on to son, bestowing his simple equipment, his tools and his cunning. May it long continue, and so help preserve that skill and enterprise which was the basis of all our crafts, as chair-bodging must really be the foundation of the rise to greatness of High Wycombe itself.

It was a pleasant surprise to find these chair-bodgers in the woods about Speen were comparatively young men. One was 48 and the other 41. Their old shanty housed two pole-lathes, the butts of the saplings sticking out, one through the doorway, the other through the window, and tethered to posts in a most inconsequential manner. All around was littered with shavings and chippings, old wooden implements, logs and arboreal trimmings. I watched the turner standing with his back to the dim and bosky light, working the V-shaped hazel foot-pedal, peeling off delicate creamy ribbons from the spinning billet, in a setting that carried the picture from Birket Foster to Rembrandt. They worked nine or ten hours a day, and could each make ten dozen legs in a day.

At one time they felled the trees themselves, but this is now left to the woodmen, and they take the tree where felled, cut it into convenient lengths, and carry the logs to their hut. The logs are then cleft by means of beetle and wedge, the clefts first trimmed with a side-axe, then worked up on the shaving horse with the draw-knife (*Fig.* 88), and finally turned on the pole-lathe, cutting on the inward turn, all in the green state. They are then stacked in neat piles outside, and covered over with a piece of corrugated-iron to dry, although they are finally dried in the factories before incorporation into chairs.

The tools are simple—a splitting axe, roughly shaped beetles, a felling axe, and on the more primitive of the two beetles, a short-handled side-axe, and a draw-knife.

The side-axe, which in this case is not a true one, is of great interest. It is sharpened on one side only, and is amongst man's most primitive tools, for it was largely used, with the adze, by mediaeval builders in shaping the timbers for houses. My informant told me they are difficult to obtain now. They are also used in the making of cricket bats.

And that is all, but with these tools and the skill which employs them, comes that beautiful but enigmatic entity—the Windsor Chair. That it was born in a wood to supply man's elemental need of a seat is all that can be said; and that is enough. It was certainly valued by our ancestors, and found its way to the New World where a Colonial variant set its roots and flourished exceedingly. An advertisement of 1730 tells of 'all sorts of Windsor Garden Chairs of all sizes, painted green or in the wood, at John Brown's, at the Three Chairs and Walnut Tree in St. Paul's Church Yard, near the School.'

In the old days many of the chair-bodgers also made the chairs, but for the most part this was a separate industry, and its home was High Wycombe. Here, today, behind many of the modern factories are the old weather-boarded lofts where the firm in question first began. And here also are to be found a number of old craftsmen who refuse to give up, finding a delight in carrying on, proud of their calling and their record. In many cases these men have relatives or brothers who still do the bodging, and it was by one of these I was directed to seek his brothers in the woods at Speen, not far from Disraeli's Hughenden.

And how proud the chair-maker was of his tools that littered the benches of the old wooden-walled building, while overhead and on the walls hung the moulds or templates of traditional patterns in backs, legs and balusters.

Like most woodworkers he always aspired to make his own, and those shown in the photograph (*Fig.* 87) are all hand-made except the two metal braces. They are as follows—three wooden braces (sways in Suffolk), the one top left, being fitted with a spoon-bit and used for cutting the mortises for the bow and the sticks in the backs of Windsor chairs. This work calls for considerable skill as each dowel enters the bow at a different angle. Then follows the two examples of steel braces which are early ones, the bits being held by thumb-screws. All these were used in conjunction with a breast-bib, which was a hollowed wooden cup, fastened to the chest of the craftsman by means of which he could press his body's weight on the bit. These bibs were also used on the heads of unruly apprentices to keep them in order. Below these are calipers or dividers, used for measuring distances on chairs.

Of the four remaining tools, the top two are travishers, for finishing off the elm seats after adzing; the top one being placed edge-wise to show the fine curve. Then comes a stock-scraper or scarifier for cleaning up surfaces of a chair frame; and finally a rebating knife for making the rebate of a chair seat ready for caning.

The late George Goodchild, of Knap Hill Common, Bucks, has been described as the very last of the old chair-bodgers. He was of those who felled the trees and made up the chair completely to the finishing, using only hand-tools and the pole-lathe. He created a tool of his own, which he dubbed—'my tool'. This consisted of a bit fashioned from a one-inch flat file, set in a handle like a large awl, with lugs at the middle. This he used as a heavy screw-driver, reamer, side-edge chisel, scriber a narrow chisel in turnery and a parting tool. He died in September, 1951, at a ripe old age.

TWENTY-ONE

THE KING'S HIGHWAY

VICTORIAN roads, dusty, gritty and strewn with horse-droppings, were dirty, slushy highways especially in the towns. The great main roads, however, after centuries of gay life in coach and wagon, posting-horse, barouche, whiskey and phaeton, suddenly died as the railways spread their network over the countryside. In short, our roads have sustained many vicissitudes, until they have arrived at their present crowded and dangerous condition.

Until the advent of tarmac the road surface was always a problem. First, the ruts and holes that must have made a journey a hazard; then the dust and grit that became mud or was swept up by any gust of wind into a penetrating cloud. And they were generally noisy, not without music, as the horses' hooves clip-clopped along, and the iron rims of the ponderous or spidery wheels ground on their way.

Packmen, pedlars, tinkers, travellers, beggars, trudged on foot, while the more advantaged, including the couriers, used their horses. And ever lurking in the background were the foot-pads and the highwaymen. Surely the most picturesque of all the cavalcade must have been the Wagons, or Carriers' Carts, with their teams of horses, sometimes as many as sixteen, huge tilts, and ponderous straked wheels. They trudged on through the night, linking town with town.

The most interesting of the country institutions in

this realm were the carriers and their carts. These linked up the villages—some of them very outlying—with the small market towns, just as the wagons linked up the Metropolis with the provincial towns. They were ubiquitous, carrying not only goods, but all kinds of passengers, and one wonders how the horses stood it. In nearly every case the driver-also-owner was a character, and he carried that less bulky but far more uncertain quantity—news and letters.

Market-Day was their great event. On the outward journey, calling at most inns of repute, and passing less fortunate poor women carrying their baskets on arm or head, they would be loaded to capacity with farmers' wives complete with umbrellas, and their baskets slung on the axletree below. They completely filled the cart, and the smaller folk scrambled over one another. The air was filled with the babel of voices, tongues clacking faster than the pace of the poor old ambling mare.

Arrived, these women would take their stance in the Market Place, and their wares be duly displayed. And what wares! Chickens, geese, butter, eggs, bacon, fruit and vegetables in season, and not least, flowers. And all of the primest, butter perchance by the pint or yard, and various by-products of the pig, and certainly country sausages.

In all probability they would be sold out by mid-day, and if not they would dispose of the remainders to dealers or higglers, known as badgers. And after a meal of their own making they would turn to do their shopping. All the drapery and domestic establishments would be visited, and their purchases would be sent by errand boys (who were legion), to 'Mrs. Farmer's Wife', at The Bugle, c/o Turner the Carrier. And then at the appointed hour they would return to whence they came so early that morning. The carrier's horse would be harnessed up in the inn yard, all the passengers scramble in, the purchases safely stowed in the baskets that in the morning held the produce, and home they would jog.

After all, these horsed conveyances were the only means of transport, and country chapels often provided ample stabling, some of which still survives in Suffolk. Otherwise it was found at the inns, where the Ostler's Bell was marked conspicuously, and where 'Good Stabling', 'Posting', and the like were advertised. The doctor had his gig, so did the vet, the miller, the dealer; and very smart their turn-outs were. These also found baiting at the inn as occasion required.

London was always a noisy place, and its streets full. All the tradesmen had their little boxes on wheels, characteristic and traditional to their respective trades. All bowling along over the gritty roads; and some will recall that peculiar little phase when the roadway in front of a house where lay a sick person, was bedded with straw. When the necessity for this ceased I cannot say, but some lessening of the noise was observed when rubber tyres became more common, and even tradesmen adopted them, notably the milkman.

The horsed-omnibus that first appeared in July 1829, amid the howls and execrations of disgusted cabmen of Hackney origin, became an institution, and the horsed-tram not less so; while the cockaded coachman and footman lent dignity and grace to a dashing scene which a Rolls-Royce cannot achieve. And the various hand-barrows were unique if they were cumbersome, of which almost the only survivals today are the costermongers' barrows, still picturesque examples of the coach-builders' craft. The rattle of the milk-perambulators, with their jingling cans and brass churn, has given place to a mechanical carriage in which bottles rattle in metal crates.

It is a curious fact that a perambulator in which an infant could lie down did not appear on the London Streets before 1870. Prior to that various forms of children's carriages or go-carts had existed, but nothing for the infant.

The definition of perambulator given in our dictionaries is two-fold. It means one who perambulates, as well as a 'hand-carriage with three or four wheels, for one or two young children pushed from behind'. And it would appear that until quite recent years the mother in her own person performed these two functions. Like the Indians of old, she carried her child, and in her perambulations was her own perambulator!

The English model began to take shape about 1817, and was a somewhat rakish object, pulled along by a handle with a crossbar. The Great Exhibition of 1851 saw the encouragement of many novelties, and the elaboration of designs eventually to find expression in the peculiar little voitures on three wheels, iron shod, like to a travelling chair, some of which sported a sunshade or parasol stuck on a stem rising from the tiny floor (*Fig.* 94). 'Then little Constantina Wood arrived, driven up in a perambulator.' So wrote Miss Yonge to Coleridge.

The history of the perambulator follows that of the carriage: and this finds a common origin in the chariot. As we had streamlined *de luxe* models following the evolution of the motor car, so there were conveyances for children in the days of the Roman Empire. For example there was the *plostellum*, which was a small chariot—a little wain or cart—with which children amused themselves, and which was drawn by a couple of goats, or fleet-footed youths. Another was known as the

Curriculus—diminutive of *currus*. This consisted of a simple box body, made of wood, adorned with a few mouldings, and was drawn by a single, docile pony. One can well imagine how the Roman children emulated their elders, and like Jehu of old, 'drove furiously'; but one must also realise that like the chariots they were springless.

And so the tale proceeds, through Saxon times and the long, low carts, often with solid wheels, through the springless years, down to the Sedan Chair. And to that one great day of tremendous import when in 1670 steel springs for carriages were first introduced into England. Meanwhile Holland, Sweden and Russia succeeded in perfecting miniature sleighs that could be pushed over the snow and ice, to accommodate the children of the well-to do.

It must be realised that carriages of any kind were the prerogative of the wealthy. The poor must walk, or go horse or mule-back, carrying their children with them. In all probability the children were aired by means of litters, and that for many a long year.

The advent of the steel spring was a great advance in the evolution of the carriage, leading as it did to the 'C' spring, and the leather strap suspension, and thus to those delightful little creations of Whiskey, Barouche, Stanhopes and Tilburys, not forgetting the Curricle. To be followed by those perambulators, the pride of nursemaid and mother alike, seen in Kensington Gardens, and later in their decrepitude in the village streets. Perambulators were made to the model of papa's equipage by the carriage builders of Long Acre, until we find one the exact replica of a Hansom Cab appearing about 1880, complete with apron and overhead flap. It would appear that the models that adorned the Parisian streets were even more elaborate.

And if the City father had carriages for his children,

drawn from the life of his own stables, as it were, so the farmer had miniature farm wagons made for the delight and airing of his. A Norfolk Children's Cart appeared about 1800, the body of which consists of an open-work frame made of dowel sticks like the sides of a cot, and was pulled by a pole-like handle.

Various forms of baby-carriages appeared, notably the mail-cart; and certain folding varieties that are not unknown today.

The bicycle or velocipede appeared on the highway to cause serious concern to town and country alike in the Victorian era. It was really the outcome of the Dandy-Horse, first seen in France at the end of the eighteenth century. The impetus for this latter was given by the rider's feet touching the ground, alternatively pushing and being raised. Self-propulsion was next attempted by pulling levers with the hands, or treadling with the feet, which created a velocipede of three wheels; but it never became very popular because of the labour it entailed.

The bicycle proper came to England from France in 1868, consisting of two wheels of equal sizes. The rider sat on a suspended saddle and propelled himself by pressing his feet on pedals at the ends of cranks which turned the wheels. It was an advance but owing to its weight, faulty bearings, and the vibration, it earned itself the name of 'bone-shaker' (*Fig.* 90).

Then came the india-rubber tyre, also from France; and a wheel was invented, grooved to take it, the spokes made of thin steel wire. This 'tension' wheel soon superseded the old wooden-iron-tyred variety, and the penny-farthing bicycle was born. This in turn gave place to the Safety Bicycle and the pneumatic tyre invented by Mr. Dunlop, that have had various forms until their present day appearance. However, the earlier models lingered on to be greeted with shouts from rude boys, lips cupped in the hand: 'Old Iron! Never Rusts!'

Country life, shut off as it was from the outside world, was enlivened by the visits of travelling tradespeople. The seamstress or dressmaker, the tailor, the clockmaker, the chair-bottomer. The only survival of this order today is to be found in the travelling tinker, who also recanes chairs and repairs doormats (*Fig.* 89). He appears in ever new guise, often on a bicycle, the driving wheel of which he makes to turn his grindstone.

With the mechanisation of our London streets, and those of the countryside and the market towns, much of the poetry has gone out of the noise. No longer do we hear the musical calls of the various hawkers—the lavender woman, the fly-paper man, the vegetable seller, the milkman, the fishmonger; or the agitated call of the newsboy. In those days even the sweep became a Jack-in-the-Green, while now the muffin-man has ceased to ring his bell, the postman's knock is silenced, even as the stick of the lamp-lighter has ceased to burn. Only the rag-and-bone merchant sings melodiously for what must be worth its weight in gold! May his lungs increase, and his luck be fine.

One picturesque and interesting little machine, once seen on the roads, measuring out the distances, was the way-wiser, pedometer, perambulator or dimensurator (*Fig.* 93). This not only calculated distances for survey purposes, but was often called in to settle disputes, and there was one available for most parishes. Incidentally, miles have varied through the years, and the English Statute Mile of 1,760 yards was legalised in 1593. Prior to that there had been the Roman mile of 1,617 English yards, the Scottish mile of 1,976 yards, and the Irish mile of 2,240 yards.

This machine said to have been designed by John Ogilby, who introduced it when undertaking his survey of the roads of England and Wales in 1671, has a wheel diameter of 2 feet 7½ inches, equal to the land measure of half a pole. It records rods, poles and perches on one circle and miles on the other, of the little clock face fitted to the hub.

These measuring wheels were often used in the case of Post Office disputes as to porterage. One such came to light when a man who started life as a Post Office messenger told of an objection to payment made by the recipient of a telegram who lived on the edge of the mile radius, up to which a message was delivered free, but above which a charge of sixpence was made. The wheel was brought into play, and if the telegram was delivered to the back door of the house in question it was under the mile, but if to the front it was just over the mile. Needless to say, the back door was the one used.

And another, indeed the earliest form of transport, seen on the roads of old England, was the Pack-stick. This enabled balanced loads to be 'bone carted', according to colloquial language, that is on the shoulder, and must have been the sort of thing used by Dick Whittington when he came to Town. The countryman proper, would find such a stick in the hedgerow, fashioned by nature, but the one shown in Figure 91 has been bent by steaming like the walking sticks and is of ash. It calls to mind the old Yorkshire saying, as used in the York Mystery Plays—'He's a fond (silly) chapman that comes the day after the fair.'

Figure 95 shows a metal perambulator for the peddling of paraffin oil, complete with measures, once used in the streets of Bewdley, Worcestershire.

TWENTY-TWO

THE GLASS-HOUSE
POT MAKER AND HIS CRAFT

No art can with the potter's art compare,
We make our potts of what we potters are.

I WAS reminded of the above old couplet, which forms an inscription on a jug, when after some difficulty I found Charles Squires in his rambling wooden workshop at Stourbridge. One would hardly go to this border town in search of romance, yet it is there, and I felt it as I crept past an immense bottle-like structure of fireclay that cut the wintry sky with its sloping sides. A one-time familiar symbol of a factory for the making of glass-ware and known as a Glass-House, not because it is made of crystal, but rather because it held the furnace that melted the glass. And in the progress of the years, even these are discarded and remain like to the wind-mills, to be used as store-houses or not at all.

It was not far from this glass-house that I found Charles Squires, who makes by hand, with the primitive methods of all his fathers, Glass-House Pots, Skittles, Cannons and Colour Pots, all of which are used in the glass furnaces. At one time they also specialised in Crucibles, and Pot Rings, which latter are now made in the brick-fields. It was a revelation to me, walking out from the prosaic streets of a busy manufacturing town, into a border-land indeed, where yesterday with all its primitive crafts and cunning meets today and its common need. If Stourbridge is on the edge of the Black Country, looking also towards the fair lands of Worcestershire, so Charles Squires stands for the very basis of our fabric, with all its complicated and machine driven life. He is the hand-craftsman out of which all our manufactures have sprung, and the link which binds us with yesterday.

I found him a most genial and kindly man, with a pleasant smile and an almost dusty face that reminded me of a miller. My first question set him talking, for I asked him from whence he got his clay. He was quick in answering; Stourbridge Clay was good enough for him, for there is none better, and pots such as he makes must have the best. Whereas anything would do for bricks and such like, glass pots call for the finest fireclay, as free from iron and impurities as it is possible, and this is only obtained from deep mines. Which led us to processes.

This clay, which may vary in colour from black to grey, is delivered in large lumps. It is left in the weathering yard for a considerable period, when atmospheric action breaks it down into granular form. It is then transferred to the grinding mill which is set over a pit. Next it comes to the mixing pan, when grog is added to the constituent amount of 25 per cent. This latter, it should be mentioned, is clay which has been burnt in a kiln and ground up, and by this admixture undue shrinkage of the finished pot is prevented. And finally to the pug mill, from which it should emerge with the right consistency, plastic and easy to work.

In the old days it used to be trodden by the naked feet, and Charles Squires has spent many an hour doing that, but now it is done by the few mechanical aids as indicated above. The clay must be kept mellow, and this is best accomplished on a slate floor. After it leaves the pug mill it lies on these slate slabs for two or three weeks, to 'lie in sour', as my informant put it.

Tempered clay, that is, clay ready prepared for pot-making can now be obtained direct from the clay mines, which does away with the preparatory processes on the part of the potter; but like all good workmen he prefers to mix and temper his own, to his complete satisfaction.

It was a fascinating sight to see the various pots standing about in varying degrees of completion, like to some ancient Roman kiln. They are built entirely by hand, a roll of clay at a time, pressing and moulding the plastic substance to the required shape. Various moulds are used, first a jib, which is set on a turn-board, or a pot-board, then a complete section for the body of a pot, or two halves, with finally the crown turned in to form the mouth. And as each section is completed it is left to dry partially ere the next part is added, much in the same way that wattle-and-daub, cob or dry-stone walling is done.

These pots, which are oval on plan, vary in size, some being 30 inches high, by 10 inches diameter, others are 36 inches by 12 inches, 40 inches by 17 inches, and 46 inches by 20 inches. Charles Squires also makes a much larger pot, known as a Beehive because of its shape, of which he seemed very proud and only sorry that he had not one in stock to show me.

The tools are simple in the extreme, and few. They consist of clay-cutters—a segment of iron on an iron haft set in a wooden handle—wooden beaters, a jack knife or scraper—fashioned from a bedstead lath, with a curved handle—a palette knife, for cleaning off the surface of the pots as they harden, various wooden moulds for shaping the mouths of the colour pots. And I noticed hanging up amongst the trophies, a huge pair of calipers, and a bow cutting wire, fashioned like a huge and ancient bow-saw. And the rest lies in the potter's hands, supple, soft and cunning, skilled by long practice.

The firm of Squires was founded in 1830 by grandfather, whose name was Charles. He was succeeded by his son, W. H. Squires, who in turn has been succeeded by his son, another Charles. And, I am glad to say, Charles has a son who is also skilled at pot-making, but who has a farm at Clow's Top, and spends his time between the two crafts as did the earliest craftsmen, who of necessity were also tillers of the soil. The same can be said of Charles Squires, the father; when he has made enough pots to his liking, he goes off and gives his son a hand for a few weeks, returning to his first love with renewed and quickened interest.

It should be noted that these pots dry naturally and are not fired. The firing is done when they reach the glass-house and are placed in a pot-arch where they are slowly heated to the required degree. They are then transferred hot, by means of a pot-carriage to the 'eye' of the glass furnace. In the old days the pots were smoke dried by being placed on a scaffold and a smoke-fire lit underneath, the smoke filling the room. Charles Squires proudly showed me an old colour pot made by his grandfather, with the date of May 1841 scratched on it. This had been smoke dried and was cloudy in colour in consequence.

These colour pots it might be mentioned, are made in two sections, left and right, by reason of which they are also known as splits. They are fitted with a mouth set in the side at the top, fashioned by a mouth-mould. Hand-made pots are still the only means of supplying the need, and many of the large glass firms maintain their own craftsmen, like the brewers with their coopers. But experiments are being tried out in the casting of these pots, which may or may not supersede the old methods.

Anyhow Squires thought that the number of potters was on the decline.

As I paid my visit in January, I found a collection of pots standing round a home-made stove, itself made of fireclay by Squires, with a wood fire; not designed to dry the pots but to keep them free of damage by frost. They looked as though the Genii might escape at any moment; but they were the magic link as being the product of a man's hand, bringing the remote and Roman periods of our civilisation in line with this present in shape and texture.

Charles Squires works much alone; and although he is glad to talk, especially about his great art, yet he evidently takes the words of Lacordaire to heart: 'Next to speech, silence is the greatest power in the world.'

TWENTY-THREE

THE ROPER AND HIS CRAFT

May hemp bind those that honor won't.
ROPE MAKER'S MOTTO.

BEWDLEY on the banks of the Severn in Worcester-shire, with its hanging gardens, old weather-scarred red brick walls, and water-scoured ways, holds many secrets. The secrets belong to old industries and handicrafts, the ways, habits and prosperity of our fathers, and all the lore of yesterday. So old-world is its mien as one views it from the heights, or standing on Telford's Bridge, that no surprise would be felt if an ancient trow sailed by on the broad bosom and tied up at the staithe. One would take it all as a matter of course and watch for the next.

But Bewdley has a suburb, as one might expect of such a good port and prosperous hithe, and that suburb is Wribbenhall on the opposite bank of the river. Here are unique tall houses with sharp gables, and here were the warehouses that once held the corded bales. And here, tucked away in a corner beneath the railway viaduct and behind an inn that still advertises home-brewed beer under faded paint, is the home of probably the last of the Bewdley industries, that of rope-making.

The sign on the arch over the gateway as one enters describes it as a 'Rope and Twine Manufactory. Established 1801.' And within you discover not one rope-walk, but two or three side by side, set amid fruit trees and flowers. The atmosphere and character are that of a century ago, and the homely, family nature of the business is suggested by old Victorian photographs preserved in the office. One of these shows Uncle Edmund, a stout old yeoman with splendid beard, and his dog 'Roper', standing there among his men, so proud of the fine clean new ropes that are glistening as they dry in the summer's sun that has long since set.

I was reminded of the now vanished rope-walk at Southwold, Suffolk, which at times was haunted by an old dead employee. His ghost came there in the dread hours and did a turn of duty, the only instance that I can recall of such a visitor being useful.

There have been other rope-walks in Wribbenhall, running along the bank-side, but this is the only one that has survived. Indeed it is perhaps the only one left in England that will take on a special job of a short length of cord or twine to special requirements that must be made by hand. At one time the river traffic called for much of its output, but now all it can make, and more, goes to supply the needs of the carpet industry at nearby Kidderminster.

Littered about these walks is much of the old equipment that first came into use when the business was started, and even yet finds an occasional resurrection to usefulness in the making of special orders. In reality there is a dual make-up here, for whereas it has not discarded its old hand-working equipment, so also it has installed the latest machinery for coping with modern needs. Here can be made in the old, old way that peculiar need, whether it be a bell-rope, sash-cord or fishing-line, while the machines rattle off the cords and twines at top speed.

It was only yesterday that the old steam-engine was discarded, installed in 1870, and the tall chimney that still carries away the smoke is dated 1871. Incidentally, and anent this engine, one usually associates ropes with being round in section, but I was shown an ancient pierced plank used in the process of making a rope square. Squares of varying size were cut in the plank, the rope forced through and thus made square in section. These squared ropes were used for water-tight packing in old engines before the modern asbestos linings were invented.

The hand processes for a coil of rope or a ball of twine were the same in essence. First the hemp, flax or jute had to be prepared into a fluffy, loose and downy condition in order for it to be spun. Take for instance the jute or hemp which arrived in bale form, this had to be broken up into serviceable lengths on an old hand-driven hemp-breaker. The one that stands in the old barn there is thought to be the only one remaining in this country (*Fig.* 98). This was often looked upon as a punishment job given to a boy if he got on the wrong side of the spinner. It consists of two iron arms around which the hemp or jute was wrapped. A fly-wheel operated by the boy moved the arms apart, thus breaking the strands. Not an easy task and only accomplished by toil and tears. These broken fragments were then dipped in grease and passed through great combs, or iron spikes set in heavy blocks, varying in gauge from coarse to fine, until the desired fluffiness of the material was gained.

Next came the spinning, done on a spinning-wheel differing from those used in a home by being set flat against a wall and turned by a boy. These wheels are made with metal rims, have strengthening metal circles and wooden spokes, slotted in a frame consisting of two wooden uprights set with a slight gap between. Above is a spring block and several wooden whorls.

The spinner with a pad of loosened hemp or jute on

his chest commenced the spinning by threading a strand into the whorl. Then, the boy turning the wheel, he walked slowly backwards paying out the thread. A length of a few feet made, he passed the thread under a bent nail set in a heavy plank fixed to the ground, known as a drag, which served to keep it slightly taut. These threads are then made up into yarn, and given a twist, either a backwards or forwards turn, or in other words a left or right twist. And in the making of a rope or twine it is the twisting that counts, these twists being set one against the other, giving strength to the cord and counterbalance, so that the finished article should lie flat and not twist itself into kinks, destroying its use. Nowadays this yarn is bought ready made in hanks, twisted left or right as required.

The yarn is then twisted or warped into a rope, cord or twine by means of jacks. (Jacks are surely common to all trades, varying in form to answer the need of each particular craft.) This is a cogged and geared wheel, on the four spokes of which are set four hooks. These hooks hold the yarns, and if four are used, one serves as a heart on which lie the other three, but if three they lie on one another (*Fig.* 99).

The varying thicknesses made the next process is polishing. Who that handles a piece of twine or rope ever imagines that it is polished ere it leaves a factory? Yet a deal of care goes into this, and if it were not so our hands would soon know. First the line is passed through water, washed and scoured, in the case of jute, in order to get off the scum and waste, then it passes through size made from sago flour, and finally through paraffin wax. This done it rests on bearers set at intervals along the rope-walk to allow it to dry. To accomplish these processes the cords are wound over grooved metal drums and passed through wooden tanks or troughs containing first the water then the size. This winding also serves to stretch the twine or ropes.

Machines, of course, do much of this work now, but it was interesting to note the lump of wax perched over the twines as they neared the finishing process. And by the time they reach the end they have been dried on the machines.

In the case of twines and small cords the next stage is balling, which is done on a machine somewhat primitive, that could be set to pack the twine into balls weighing from a quarter, rising by quarters, up to two pounds.

The old paraphernalia, of which there was much, lying in the sheds or about the walks, was full of interest. Ancient in its inception it had served its day and yet still served. Lying in one shed was a huge wain (surely a friendly word since they made ropes for wagons, claiming relationship with the old ships of the land), for winding spun yarn. It was set on an immense sloping plank, as much as one could lift off the ground, raised at the back on two small wheels. I discovered that a wain differs from a jack only in that whereas the latter is fixed the former will move along as the work requires. Then there were tops, cut out of the solid, of beech, elm or poplar, and used for cutting and stretching the ropes; portable reels, a winding crab, guides, even an old red-earthenware pot still with grease in it as used by great-grandfather. And in the old barn I even came across an ancient pair of scales, large enough to take a sack of flour, evidently used to weigh the ropes when made since ropes and twines although sold by the ball or coil are also sold by weight.

According to an old handbill this factory manufactured all kinds of cordage for carpet looms, ropes, lines, twines;

also oil cloths, rick cloths, hair cloths, clay mill banding, plaited and round sash lines and nets. They also dealt in coco-matting, thatching yarn, door mats, garden mats, pitch, tar and oakum.

And somehow one felt that here in these old sheds and along these walks yesterday and to-day were running hand in hand, each respecting and complementing the other, with a foreman in charge so evidently proud of his craft and as interested in the days and methods of his forerunners as he is in these present.

INDEX